**NEW ENGLAND INSTITUTE
OF TECHNOLOGY
LEARNING RESOURCES CENTER**

THE BARNYARD EPITHET
AND OTHER OBSCENITIES

THE BARNYARD EPITHET

Notes on the Chicago Conspiracy Trial

DRAWINGS BY IRENE SIEGEL

AND OTHER OBSCENITIES

J. ANTHONY LUKAS

HARPER & ROW, PUBLISHERS
New York, Evanston, and London

A portion of this book first appeared in an article in the *New York Times Magazine*.

The poem "Night Apple" by Allen Ginsberg is from *Empty Mirror: Early Poems* (New York, Corinth Books, 1961). Reprinted by permission of the publisher.

FIRST EDITION

LIBRARY OF CONGRESS CATALOG CARD NUMBER: 77–128400

LEONARD WEINGLASS, a defense attorney: Mr. Schaller, is it an obscenity for the mayor of a major metropolitan area to advise his police to shoot to kill all arsonists and shoot to maim all looters?

RICHARD SCHULTZ, a government attorney: Objection.

THE COURT: I sustain the objection.

MR. WEINGLASS: Do you consider it an obscenity for the United States Government to use napalm in the bombing of civilians in North Vietnam?

MR. SCHULTZ: Mr. Weinglass can't be serious in contending that these questions are proper on this recross-examination.

MR. WEINGLASS: That is perhaps my most serious question in this trial.

Preface

For nearly five months in the fall of 1969 and the winter of 1970, I covered the Chicago Conspiracy Trial for the *New York Times*.

On February 4, 1970, during the government's rebuttal case, Chicago's Deputy Chief of Police, James Riordan, took the witness stand. Testifying about the events in Grant Park on August 28, 1968, the chief said he had seen David Dellinger leave the park at the head of a militant group. At that, Mr. Dellinger looked up from his seat at the defense table and said, "Oh, bullshit!" Later that afternoon, Judge Julius J. Hoffman sternly reprimanded Mr. Dellinger for using "that kind of language" in court and revoked his bail for the rest of the trial.

Knowing the *Times*' sensitivity about such language, I called the National Desk and asked how they wanted to handle Mr. Dellinger's phrase. The editor on duty said he didn't think we could use it and suggested I just say "an obscenity." I objected, arguing that it wasn't, strictly speaking, an obscenity; that if we called it that most people would assume it was something much worse; and that since it was central to the day's events we ought to tell our readers just what Mr. Dellinger had said. The editor thought for a moment and said, "Why don't we call it 'a barnyard epithet'?" Everything considered, that seemed like the best solution, and that was the way it appeared in the *Times* the next morning.

When the trial ended later that month, many participants and observers began writing books. I was reluctant to join the throng. The trial seemed to me such a momentous and complex event that a good book about it would come only with the perspective of years. But in the weeks that followed I was bombarded with question about "what really happened" at the trial. Ultimately, I concluded that the Barnyard Epithet was only one of many aspects which called for fuller reporting. I have not set out to write a definitive book. The few lines that follow are intended merely to expand and enrich the trial's reporting in areas which I think are least understood. I hope they will serve as a modest contribution to the growing lore on this extraordinary event.

Chicago, June 1970   J.A.L.

THE BARNYARD EPITHET
AND OTHER OBSCENITIES

"Tell me something," Judge Julius J. Hoffman said when I called him that September for press credentials. "Do you think this is going to be the trial of the century?"

• • •

"It's going to be a combination Scopes trial, revolution in the streets, Woodstock Festival and People's Park, all rolled into one," said Abbie Hoffman.

• • •

"Chicago, September 23—City and federal authorities beefed up security today on the eve of the Chicago Conspiracy Trial. United States Marshal John Meiszner announced that federal marshals had been brought in from other cities to reinforce his regular contingent and Chicago policemen would also be deputized as marshals. Meanwhile, police have drawn up 'riot control plans' to meet expected demonstrations."

• • •

"It's going to be the most important political trial in the history of the United States," said Jay Miller, director of the Illinois Division of the American Civil Liberties Union.

• • •

"This is a criminal trial, not a political trial," said Thomas Aquinas Foran, the United States Attorney. "I intend to play it as straight as possible. They can monopolize the rhetoric. I'm interested in the jury."

1

• • •

"In choosing the eight of us, the government has lumped together all the strands of dissent in the sixties," Rennie Davis explained over lunch in a Loop restaurant. "We respond by saying the movement of the past decade is on trial here."

• • •

"Ah, it's an open-and-shut case," said the taxi driver who drove me to the Federal Building that first morning. "Those anarchists will be in jail by Christmas."

• • •

Each of us brought his own assumptions into that courtroom on September 24. Mine were formed partly by inexperience, partly by a liberal's respect for the courts and the law.

This was my first major trial. As a police reporter on the Baltimore *Sun* in 1959, I'd spent many afternoons in police courts—those shabby back rooms of station houses where bored magistrates swept rapidly through dockets crammed with petty thieves, drunks, quarreling neighbors and faithless husbands. Those slipshod hearings could hardly be called trials—certainly not justice.

Yet those dreary afternoons never really shook my faith that something approaching justice was dispensed by black-robed judges sitting in cool, marble courthouses throughout the land. And this faith attached most strongly to the federal courts, which in those years played a major role in the desegregation of the South. Headlines like "Federal Court Orders

New Georgia School Plan" or "Judge Bans Bias in Memphis Parks" helped form my view of the federal district judge as a dispassionate scholar dedicated to the law and fearlessly defiant of local pressures and politics.

That image, still lingering in my mind on the morning of September 24, was undoubtedly reinforced by my first view of Chicago's new Federal Building. Ludwig Mies van der Rohe, the late *doyen* of Chicago architects, had produced a thirty-story skyscraper, sheathed in a curtain wall of soaring steel and bronze-tinted glass, which conjured up the austere grandeur and cool dignity I associated with federal courts. And Judge Hoffman's courtroom on the twenty-third floor carried through the same theme: an expanse of brown oak paneling broken only by acoustical wood baffles, colored prints of the Founding Fathers and, high above the bench, a huge silver and black seal showing a fierce American eagle ringed by "United States District Court for the Northern District of Illinois."

• • •

The judge took his stately room seriously. On November 18, as William M. Kunstler, a defense attorney, was cross-examining a witness, the judge cut in:

THE COURT: Mr. Kunstler, there is a great architect, Mies van der Rohe, who lately left us. He designed that lectern as well as the building, and it was a lectern, not a leaning post. I have asked you to stand behind it when you question the witness.

MR. KUNSTLER: Your honor, I think the U.S. Attorney questions from this table here—

THE COURT: I don't permit lawyers to lean on that thing. I don't want you to do it. . . . That was put there

3

by the government, designed by Mr. van der Rohe, and I want you to use it for that purpose.

• • •

"Those who incite to violence should be punished whether or not freedom of speech is impaired."—Congressman Robert L. F. Sikes (Democrat, Florida), during debate on the "antiriot" provisions of the 1968 Civil Rights Act.

• • •

The defendants were being tried under the antiriot provisions of the 1968 Civil Rights Act. These provisions originated with Southern Congressmen determined to prosecute the "outside agitators" they held responsible for racial unrest. As Congressman William Colmer of Mississippi put it: "We have the leaders of SNCC and other similar organizations going around from state to state preaching Black Power and inciting riots. Here we are with one Stokely Carmichael and one Rap Brown, with headquarters down in Atlanta, Georgia, who among others we find traveling from state to state and from city to city, and in their wake comes conflagration, blood-spilling, wholesale pilfering and the loss of life and property."

Federal laws did not prohibit rioting or even incitement to riot, for those were state offenses and most states already had ample legislation against them. The new law gave the federal government a legal hook to snag the agitators as they went by: their "intent" to incite a riot as they moved from state to state.

The Justice Department did not want that hook. The then Attorney General, Ramsey Clark, felt riots were properly the responsibility of the states and localities.

4

"There are few activities that are more local," he has said. "They're right on the ground, they're out on the street someplace." Moreover, he feared that prosecutions for intent might infringe constitutionally protected rights to freedom of speech, assembly and movement. "Government," he said, "has an absolute duty to do what it can to enlarge the opportunities of its people to speak, and a bill like this does just the opposite. It makes it exceedingly dangerous."

Even after Congress passed the provisions, Clark was reluctant to use them. After the violence during the Democratic National Convention of 1968, he called U.S. Attorney Foran and ordered him to proceed cautiously, through a "lawyers' investigation" rather than with a grand jury. Apparently, he was chiefly interested in prosecuting the police for brutality.

When word of this got to Chicago's Mayor Richard J. Daley, he was outraged. Stung by widespread criticism of his hard-line tactics during the convention, he wanted vindication and revenge on the radicals who had dared to challenge him. So the Daley machine ground smoothly into operation. Chief Federal District Judge William Campbell, long a close friend of the mayor, summoned a grand jury and instructed it to look specifically for violations of the antiriot law. Mr. Foran, who owed his appointment directly to the mayor, came up with supporting evidence, and on March 20, 1969, the jury returned indictments against eight demonstrators neatly balanced by eight policemen.

By this time, the Nixon Administration was in Washington. The reluctant Mr. Clark had been replaced by John Mitchell, who was publicly proclaiming his eagerness to go after radicals with every instrument at his disposal. Seeing that his interests neatly

the judge

coincided with Mr. Daley's in this case, he gave the final go-ahead for prosecution.

• • •

ABBIE HOFFMAN: Are you asking if I had those thoughts or if I wrote that I had those thoughts? There's a difference.

RICHARD G. SCHULTZ, THE ASSISTANT U.S. ATTORNEY: It's a convenient difference, isn't it, Mr. Hoffman?

ABBIE: I don't know what you mean. I've never been on trial for my thoughts before.

• • •

The law bothered me because I didn't know how to judge any man's intent, much less these men's.

Once I had been asked to do just that. In the summer of 1968, plans for protest during the Democratic convention were being announced almost daily. My editors needed some estimate of what might happen so they could decide how to deploy their own forces during convention week. I was sent to Chicago to find out what the demonstrators intended.

At that time, of course, nobody had isolated the eight men who were to be on trial. I sought out all the dissidents: the S.D.S., the Coalition for an Open Convention, the McCarthy kids and a group allegedly planning a march of bare-breasted maidens down Michigan Avenue. But I did talk with Rennie Davis and Tom Hayden in the chaotic Loop offices of the Mobilization Committee to End the War in Vietnam; I sat on the grass in Lincoln Park with Lee Weiner and John Froines while the demonstration "marshals" practiced snake dances and skirmish lines on the baseball field;

7

I heard Jerry Rubin expound plans for the Yippie "festival of life"; and I joined Abbie Hoffman as he led his police tails on a wild chase across the North Side.

The more I talked with them, the more unsure I was just what they intended. All the demonstrators, of course, wanted to make an effective protest against the war, racism and the unresponsiveness of the Democratic party. But there were wide differences about whether an effective protest would be helped or hindered by confrontations in the street. On the one hand, violence or the threat of violence would frighten away many of the demonstrators the leaders hoped to attract. On the other hand, police action—especially if it was brutal, as it was almost bound to be in Chicago—was the best way of radicalizing people and pointing up the "repressiveness" of the state. Most of those I talked to saw both points and, I think, often vacillated between them.

Over lunch one day, Rennie Davis conceded he would like to see pictures on the front page of every newspaper in the country the day after Humphrey was nominated showing the International Amphitheater ringed by tanks, barbed wire and soldiers with bayonets. "It'll show the Democrats can't hold a convention without calling in the army," he said.

"Wouldn't it be even more effective if the soldiers shot a little girl?" I asked. "Or two girls? Or twenty? Wouldn't that radicalize the McCarthy kids a lot quicker?"

"Perhaps," he said. "But we don't need that. We're not after bloodshed. A symbolic confrontation will make the point."

I looked across the table at the disarming young man who always reminded me of a Kansas 4-H leader but who I knew was a shrewd, resourceful radical. Was I being taken in? How much of the truth was I getting? I was never sure.

Now, thirteen months later, I wondered how a jury could possibly make that delicate judgment.

• • •

MR. SCHULTZ: You practice shooting an M-1, don't you?

LINDA MORSE: Yes, I do.

MR. SCHULTZ: You also practice karate, don't you?

LINDA MORSE: Yes, I do . . .

MR. SCHULTZ: That is for the revolution, isn't it?

LINDA MORSE: After Chicago, I changed from being a pacifist to the realization we had to defend ourselves. A nonviolent revolution was impossible. I desperately wish it was possible.

• • •

Nobody in that courtroom was the same person he had been thirteen months before. Nobody had the same intentions.

Linda Morse's tale of lightning conversion from pacifism to violent revolution may be a little hard to accept. But many young people who crossed state lines on their way to Chicago, believing that nonviolent protest could be effective, crossed them going back full of doubt. And Nixon's election, the new hard line at the Justice Department, the continuing slaughter in Vietnam only pushed people further into an apocalyptic rhetoric I found dangerous and self-defeating.

Some of the defendants had clearly moved far in that direction. Others seemed skeptical about much of the new mood. After all, they were an older generation—most hovering about thirty, one fifty-four—bred in an earlier, more optimistic stage of the Movement. But precisely because they were now almost elder statesmen of the New Left—regarded as irrelevant by some young radicals—they could not afford to be left behind.

This was clear enough during the Weathermen's "Days of Rage" in Chicago in October 1969. Privately, several defendants told me they were unhappy about the windshield-busting rampage through the streets. But, at news conferences, they refused to distance themselves from the young street fighters. As one defendant put it: "When the Movement is embattled, you don't start denouncing your brothers."

And it became even clearer later. On March 13, during a wave of bombings and bomb scares in New York, Abbie Hoffman encouraged students at Columbia University to experiment further with such "better living through chemistry." Four days later, Rennie Davis told another audience at Columbia that if the nineteen-sixties were a decade for sit-ins, the seventies were a time to "burn the banks."

Irresponsible though such statements might be, could the government really prove the defendants' states of mind in August 1968 through statements they made more than a year later? Two of Abbie Hoffman's speeches in the fall of 1969—one allegedly urging the firebombing of police cars—were introduced by the government during its rebuttal case.

The defendants' states of mind in the fall of 1969 had also been profoundly influenced by the outcome of the Spock trial. The baby doctor and his four co-defendants, accused of conspiring to counsel draft evasion, conducted a cautious, by-the-book defense, sticking to legal questions, eschewing the broad political issues and making no effort to stir up support outside the courtroom. They were convicted anyway (although the convictions were overturned on appeal). Dr. Spock said later: "We sat like good little boys called into the principal's office. I'm afraid we didn't prove very much."

From the start, the Chicago defendants rejected a narrow Spock defense. If their stance had a precedent, it was far more the Huey P. Newton and Oakland Seven trials, in which the defense staged the fight on openly political grounds.

But here the defendants did more than merely accept the government's challenge to a political trial. They welcomed it. There wasn't much going on in the radical movement, anyway. The S.D.S. was hopelessly splintered and ineffective. Winter was coming on and there wouldn't be any campus uprisings for a while. So the defendants determined to make the trial the central radical event of the year. They saw it as an opportunity to radicalize people around the issues of the courts and the law.

• • •

"The Conspiracy in the streets needs: freedom, actors, peace, turf, money, sunshine, musicians, instruments, people, props, cars, air, water, costumes, sound equipment, love, guns, freaks, friends, anarchy, Huey free, a truck, airplanes, power, glory, old clothes, space, truth, Nero, paint, help, rope, swimming hole, ice cream, dope, nookie, moonship, Om, lords, health, no hassles, land, pigs, time, patriots, spaccsuits, a Buick, people's justice, Eldridge, lumber, panthers, real things, good times."—Leaflet handed out by the Conspiracy office in the week before the trial.

11

• • •

To conspire means "to breathe together." By that, or any other standard, it is hard to imagine these eight men conspiring. "Conspire, hell," Abbie Hoffman once said. "We couldn't agree on lunch."

In the mock "program" for the trial ("The Chicago Conspiracy vs. The Washington Kangaroos"), six of the Conspiracy team were listed as quarterbacks (Lee Weiner was "left fielder" and John Froines "lonesome end"). That was all too appropriate, for none of these men was about to let any other call the signals. If it was a team at all, it had the most hybrid line-up on record:

TOM HAYDEN: If they were to be ranked by sheer intelligence, perhaps Hayden would have to come first. He is hardly impressive looking with his acne-scarred face and bulbous nose (which Nick von Hoffman said made him look like "a bankrupt, alcoholic pilgrim or English village lout"); but what a policewoman called his "beady eyes" size up the world with penetrating keenness. Widely regarded as the Movement's chief ideologue, he drafted its most famous declaration— the 1962 Port Huron Statement, which gave voice to the open idealism of the early New Left ("we regard men as infinitely precious, possessed of unfulfilled capacities for reason, freedom, love"). Most of this optimistic glow has been seared out of him by beatings and cold jail cells in the South, the misery he saw in Newark's black ghetto and the firsthand evidence of American militarism he picked up on two trips to North Vietnam. After the Chicago convention, he went off to form the Berkeley Liberation School, where he frankly called for revolution. Yet, always the most coolly analytical of revolutionaries, Hayden had none

12

tom hayden

of the martyr's zeal evident in some of the others. He believed a revolutionary's chief duty was to stay out of jail and on the streets where he could be effective. Perhaps his zest for freedom stemmed in part from the lovely blond California girl who waited for him on the relatives' bench. After he was sentenced to five years in prison, Hayden told the court he regretted the punishment because he "would like to have a child." When Judge Hoffman cut in to say "there is where the federal system can do you no good," Hayden shot back "the federal system can do you no good in trying to prevent the birth of a new world."

• • •

RENNIE DAVIS: My hunch about Rennie's 4-H background proved correct. He first came to Chicago for a 4-H chicken-judging contest and won fourth prize. Since then he had turned his talents to the Movement, developing into its leading Organization Man. Impressive academic credentials—B.A., Oberlin; M.A., University of Illinois; further graduate work at Michigan —would have paved his way into many other endeavors; but by the mid-sixties he had become one of the first full-time Movement bureaucrats, working with S.D.S., its Economic Research and Action Projects, Chicago's JOIN community union and then the Mobilization Committee to End the War in Vietnam. Already based in Chicago, he was a natural choice to become codirector (with Hayden) of the convention demonstration. He did most of the real organizing that summer and then played much the same role in the trial-time Conspiracy office. By the time he took the witness stand late in the trial, he had let his hair curl down over the collar of his checked wool shirts, and

14

he looked a little less like a student council president; but his wholesome air and wide-eyed answers infuriated the prosecutors, who complained that he was putting on a "little boy next door" act for the jury. And sure enough, once he was sentenced to prison, he turned quite a different tone on the government table: "When I come out of prison it will be to move next door to Tom Foran. I am going to be the boy next door. The boy that could have been a judge, the boy that could have been a prosecutor, could have been a college professor, is going to move next door to organize his kids into the revolution. We are going to turn the sons and daughters of the ruling class in this country into Viet Cong."

• • •

DAVID DELLINGER: Fifty-four, chubby, nearly always dressed in the same green-tweed sports jacket and rumpled flannels, Dellinger looked like an off-duty scoutmaster. Amid that riotous profusion of hair, his few jagged straw-colored swatches were folded across his balding dome like a carelessly repaired thatch roof. Politically, too, he was an anachronism: an evangelical Christian Socialist among New Leftists who flaunted their agnosticism and celebrated their liberation from outworn dogmas. Yet there was nothing prim or flabby about Dave's brand of radicalism. Bred on the stony soil of Wakefield, Massachusetts, and raised a Congregationalist, he quickly developed a stern, even rigid sense of rectitude. After graduating from Yale (in the same class with Walt Rostow and Stewart Alsop), he was studying for the ministry at Union Theological Seminary when World War II broke out. As a seminarian, he could have had a draft defer-

15

ment, but he refused to register and was sent to prison for a year. On his release, he again refused to register and was sent back for two more years (and promptly staged a sixty-day hunger strike). Ever since, he has remained the most active of pacifists—protesting the Korean War, the Bay of Pigs and finally emerging as chairman and moving spirit behind the National Mobilization Committee to End the War in Vietnam. This earned him the government's tag as "chief architect" of the convention conspiracy, a title he publicly laughed off but secretly seemed to cherish. For his bedrock convictions and determination to resist authority he considered illegitimate made him the most stubbornly combative—and least subtle or pragmatic —of all the defendants. Some of the others winced when Dave rose to call Judge Hoffman a "liar," a "fascist" and "the chief prosecutor," or when he blurted out the Barnyard Epithet.

• • •

ABBIE HOFFMAN: Who was Abbie? His very identity became an issue in the trial. Was he, as the indictment alleged, Abbott H. Hoffman, a leader of the Youth International Party? Or was he, as he insisted on the witness stand, just Abbie, an orphan of America and a child of the Woodstock Nation? Part of this was a mere word game with the other Hoffman: Abbie called the judge his "illegitimate father" and said he was publicly renouncing the name Hoffman. But part of it was all too serious: reflecting Abbie's conviction that identity—and reality—are defined by myth artfully propagated through the media. Abbie's prime myth that winter was the Woodstock Nation. When asked where it was, he explained: "It is a nation of

16

alienated young people. We carry it around with us as a state of mind in the same way the Sioux Indians carried the Sioux nation around with them. It is a nation dedicated to cooperation versus competition, to the idea that people should have better means of exchange than property or money, that there should be some other basis for human interaction. . . ." On a more literal level, Abbie comes from Worcester, Massachusetts, breezed through Brandeis in white tennis sneakers, worked in H. Stuart Hughes' 1962 peace campaign for the Senate, served as a psychologist at Worcester State Hospital and then plunged into SNCC activity in the South. He was still a rather straight young man when he came to New York in 1966, turned onto drugs and gradually distilled the peculiar blend of street theater, confrontation and put-on which he calls "monkey warfare" (Jack Newfield calls him "a pure Marxist-Lennonist—Harpo Marx and John Lennon"). For most of the trial, Abbie suffered from a lingering Chicago winter cold which kept him bleary-eyed and sniffly, but even off his best form he was the most consistently intriguing figure in the courtroom. There was a touch of genius in his mock-Olympic leap over the velvet rope on the center aisle; in his solemn conclusion that one of Judge Hoffman's rulings was the worst he'd heard "in all my years on the witness stand"; and in his simple admonition to his wife as he was being led off to jail: "Water the plant."

•   •   •

JERRY RUBIN: Jerry tried hard to be the fighting man's Abbie. He carefully nurtured his Yippie image, buying a bushy wig to cover his prison-sheared head,

17

wearing bright corduroy pants and polo shirts speckled with buttons, bantering brightly with marshals and spectators. But he never quite brought it off. The zany, zonked-out style couldn't cover the hard, knotted roots of Jerry's radicalism, which probably reached back to his childhood days in Cincinnati. The son of a bakery driver turned Teamsters official, he grew up feeling snubbed and patronized by his four uncles, the affluent, suburban Katz brothers. "My whole life," he once said, "has been a battle of the Rubins against the Katzes." The battle carried him first to quick prominence as the youth-page editor of the Cincinnati *Post,* to Israel where he studied sociology, to Berkeley where he joined the Free Speech Movement and ran for mayor, then on to become project director for the March on the Pentagon. With the emergence of hippies and the drug culture, Jerry sought an amalgam of political and personal liberation—producing Yippie and the Chicago "festival of life." But there was really nothing very lighthearted about Jerry. At one of the trial's most dramatic moments, he marched back and forth in front of the bench, his arm thrust up in the Nazi salute, shouting "Heil Hitler." At times, as the verdict approached, he looked positively frightened. But at the end he managed to muster a tight little grin as he told the judge, "We're going to jail with smiles on our faces because we know that there are millions of young kids out there who identify with us and are going to fight to free us, and that's the revolution." Then, in a typically Rubinesque flourish, he pulled out a still-unbound copy of his book (a dozen had been rushed to Chicago especially for the occasion), autographed it and handed it up to the judge.

• • •

JOHN FROINES: On the day he handed out contempt citations, Judge Hoffman started to deal with the defense attorneys, then looked up and caught himself: "Oh, I beg your pardon, I almost forgot to take care of Mr. Froines." John Froines smiled ruefully as he remarked: "It's part of being a media unknown that even the judge finally forgets you're here." Through most of the trial, John bore his obscurity with good grace, ceding the floor on public and private occasions to the better-known defendants. He dressed simply in open-necked sports shirts and wash pants; perhaps his most distinctive feature was his bristling but well-trimmed gold mustache. Yet I liked John immensely. He had a quiet, gentle irony which slipped out in brief corridor colloquies. One day, I asked tongue-in-cheek whether he could really make the stink bombs he was alleged to have manufactured during convention week. The next morning, in court, he handed me a reprint of a journal article he had written entitled: "Luminescence of Paracyclophanes L. Syn-And Anti-(2.2) Paracyclonaphthane." Judging by his record, John is a chemist of some distinction. He holds degrees from Berkeley (B.A.) and Yale (M.A., Ph.D.), did postdoctoral research on a National Institutes of Health fellowship at the Royal Institution of Great Britain and is now assistant professor of chemistry at the University of Oregon. At Yale he was chairman of Students for Johnson in the 1964 election, but soon moved into S.D.S., serving for two years as a community organizer in its New Haven community project. Later, he was a cofounder of the Radical Science Information Service, which helps "scientists of a radical bent make explicit connections about science and society." John had made his connections. When the judge finally got around to citing him for

20

contempt, John stood and read a section from the Oregon constitution, pausing to emphasize the part which said the people "have at all times a right to alter, reform or abolish the government in a manner as they may think proper."

• • •

LEE WEINER: Lee was the Conspiracy's odd-man-out, a strangely remote figure who shunned most of the defendants' extracurricular activities. From the start, he seemed convinced they were all doomed to conviction, and he didn't like the attorneys to raise false hopes with talk of possible acquittal. Instead of attending the interminable defense strategy sessions, he hurried home to the South Side apartment he shared with a kooky young art dealer named Sharon. At the defense table, Lee generally kept his head deep in a book—Lao-tzu's works, the *I Ching*, Matza's *Becoming Deviant* and a whole host of science fiction paper-backs. Once, while a witness was describing how non-violent Lee was, I looked up to find him immersed in Von Clausewitz's *On War*. He rarely reacted to what went on in court, except when one of the prosecutors pronounced his name—as they invariably did— W*ee*ner. Then he would look up for a moment, fix the offender with an exasperated glare and say W*i*ner. He seemed to regard the proceedings with a mixture of arch amusement and scathing scorn. Once, when a prosecutor called Rennie Davis a "split personality," Lee chuckled softly and said "now he's a psychological student." Lee was very much the student—a doctoral candidate and teaching assistant in sociology at North-western. With his bushy black beard and steel-rimmed glasses, he looked like he'd just emerged from the

21

cubicle next to Karl Marx at the British Museum. But he had a nice Jewish sense of the incongruity of his position. Once he wrote: "I never wanted to be a doctor, but after a while I accumulated a bunch of university degrees, and now I'm going to get another that will mean terrorized freshmen will call me 'doctor' on their bad days. It makes my mother happy. . . . [I also have] a tattoo on my forehead that says 'Government Certified Radical.' If I stay in touch with myself and continue to act free, the government has promised to additionally tattoo in 'Bomb Maker and Evil Man.' It makes me happy."

• • •

BOBBY SEALE: When Bobby was led into the courtroom that first morning, several of the defendants barely knew him. For if a conspiracy existed during convention week, he was at most its imported West Coast talent, brought in as a last-minute speaking replacement for Eldridge Cleaver. He took part in none of the advance planning, stayed barely forty-eight hours, gave only two speeches. Those first days in the courtroom I thought I caught a quizzical look in his eyes, as though he were asking himself, "What the hell am I doing here?" After all, he was facing a much more serious charge—conspiracy to commit murder—in Connecticut, which kept him imprisoned every night and weekend while he was in Chicago. Each morning, when the guards brought him to court, the other defendants and their lawyers greeted him warmly, handing him mail and newspaper clippings, trying to make him feel part of the team. But Bobby held them off, sitting a little apart at the table, rarely taking part in the football-huddle conferences, signi-

22

fying his approval or disapproval with curt nods. In sleek turtleneck shirts, his taut figure commanded respect, even from his antagonists (after the trial Tom Foran said Seale had "more guts and charisma than any of them"). There were those who suspected his solitary stance might be chiefly trial strategy, but then he really was different: the black son of a Texas carpenter; a sheet-metal mechanic; funky jazz drummer; stand-up comedian; veteran of ghetto skirmishes with the police; cofounder of the Black Panther Party; and now (with Cleaver and Huey P. Newton in jail or in flight) the party's national chairman. But I didn't realize just how different he was until he came back late in the trial to testify as a defense witness, and the government confronted him with taped recordings of the two speeches he gave those days in Chicago. They contained passages like these: "Pick up a gun and pull that spike out from the wall. Because if you pull it on out and if you shoot well, all I'm gonna do is pat you on the back and say 'keep on shooting.'" And, "If the police get in the way of our march, tangle with the blue-helmeted motherfuckers and kill them and send them to the morgue slab."

• • •

When the three hundred members of the September venire filed into the courtroom on the second day of the trial they were so overwhelmingly white, middle-class and middle-aged they looked like the Rolling Meadows Bowling League lost on their way to the lanes.

The defense contended that the venire, selected from the voter registration list, automatically excluded the young, unsettled, black and alienated—precisely

23

those to whom the defendants appealed most. Antici-
pating that this objection would be rejected, it submitted forty-four questions designed to smoke out the
prejudices lurking among the prospective jurors. They
included:

"Do you believe that Martin Luther King, Jr.,
should have come to Chicago in 1967 to lead demon-
strations?"
"Do you know who Janis Joplin and Jimi
Hendrix are?"
"Have you or any members of your family ever
displayed a placard or bumper sticker reading: 'Sup-
port Your Local Police'?"
"Would you let your son or daughter marry a
Yippie?"
"If your children are female, do they wear bras-
sieres all the time?"

Judge Hoffman refused to ask all but one of the
defense's questions: "Are you, or do you have any
close relatives or friends who are, employed by any
law-enforcement agencies or other agencies of the
local, state or federal government?" This—and a few
perfunctory questions about the prospective jurors'
professions and families—exhausted the judge's examination.

The government used peremptory challenges to
knock off two jurors who seemed risky: a June graduate of the University of Illinois and a Negro just laid
off after thirty-one years as a Pullman porter. The
defense challenged a semiretired man named Woj-
chiechowski, the daughter of a veteran Chicago policeman, an employee of the Federal Aviation Agency and
a man who belonged to a club made up primarily of
policemen.

24

david dellinger

And there—in less than three hours—was the jury: two middle-aged white men, two Negro women and eight white women, most of them suburban housewives and widows. Perhaps not the worst jury that could have been drawn from that venire, I thought; but were the defendants really getting a jury of their peers?

• • •

After the verdict, one of the jurors told the Chicago *Sun-Times* that two of her colleagues "expressed the view that the young people who demonstrated during the convention should have been shot down by the police." One of them was "convinced that the defendants should be convicted because of their appearance, their language and their life style." When challenged by the other jurors, she kept asking: "Would you like your children to grow up that way?"

Edward Kratzke, the foreman, said, "I was a streetcar conductor. I've seen guys, real bums with no soul, just a body, but when they went in front of a judge they had their hats off. These defendants wouldn't even stand up when the judge walked in. When there is no more respect we might as well give up the United States."

Another juror, Mrs. Ruth Petersen, told an interviewer that her gravest fear during the trial was that her eighteen-year-old son, a college freshman, might become a hippie. Of the defendants, she said: "They needed a good bath and to have their hair cut. . . . They had no respect for nobody, not even the marshals. When they told them to get their feet off their chairs, they just put them right back up again. I don't think that's nice."

• • •

The defendants' manners weren't always nice. They did put their booted feet up on the black leather chairs, and sometimes even on the table. The radicals wore blue jeans and sweat shirts which sometimes rode above the waist to expose a hairy belly or scrawny back. The Yippies wore a dazzling and constantly changing array of brightly striped polo shirts, corduroy or leather pants, sashes, headbands, beads and buttons. As the proceedings droned on, they read newspapers, books, memos and mail; wrote speeches and press releases; munched jelly beans; whispered; made faces; snickered or dozed. The defense table—actually four Formica-topped tables pushed together—looked like a college administration building after a four-day siege, a "liberated zone" right there in the courtroom. It and the carpet around were littered with papers, candy wrappers, sweaters, boots and leather jackets— even, one day, a package of marijuana.

Across the narrow aisle, the government's table reproached us all with its cool, efficient order. The gleaming surface was never marred by more than a few neatly stacked memos and a spare pencil or two, but a formidable array of carefully indexed cardboard files stood on a gray steel trolley at one end. The prosecution team always sat in a precise symmetrical pattern: Tom Foran and his assistant, Dick Schultz, on one side, facing Roger Cubbage, a Justice Department attorney and Joseph Stanley, an F.B.I. man—all four in neatly creased gray, brown or olive-drab business suits (never a pattern bolder than a pin stripe), their narrow ties anchored with small gold tacks.

One girl who attended the trial frequently said the two tables seemed locked in a battle between "sex and sterility." That may be overstating it, but the struggle did have its sexual overtones. The defense staff boasted several attractive young women who often sat in the front row of the press section, mini-skirted and braless, laughing appreciatively at the defendants and hissing the government attorneys. Wives and girl friends showed up regularly, exchanging meaningful glances with their inamoratos. Lee Weiner and Sharon solved their courtroom communications problem by learning sign language and flashing undecipherable messages back and forth all day. Lee and Sharon hugged a lot too and didn't care who watched. As court adjourned on New Year's Eve, they passed out autographed posters of themselves in a naked embrace under the slogan: "Make a New Year's Revolution, Kids. It'll Bring You Closer Together."

This sort of thing obviously bothered the prosecutors, who had few supporters, masculine or feminine, in the courtroom. (Their wives came only rarely.) Mr. Foran objected strenuously to the defendants' courtroom "claque." Once, when Susan Schultz, Rennie Davis's girl friend, came over for a cozy courtroom conference with Rennie, Mr. Foran jumped up and asked that the defendants "try to look a little less like we are sitting in a living room in front of the fire. We have had a young lady kneeling with her arms in his lap. This is a federal courthouse, Your Honor." They were also unnerved by the uninhibited affection which many of the defendants, their lawyers and the male staff members showed for each other. (It bothered His Honor too. Once, he admonished Mr. Kunstler: "I have never presided at a trial where there is so much physical affection demonstrated in the courtroom. . . . Perhaps this is part of a love-in.")

• • •

The government lost no opportunity for parading

the defendants' "obscenities" before the jury. Over and over, the prosecutors or government witnesses repeated the Anglo-Saxon terms they said they had heard Jerry Rubin or Abbie Hoffman use.

The police witnesses who took the stand were sometimes almost prissy. Barbara Callender, a red-headed policewoman who had posed as a hippie in Lincoln Park during the convention, testified that "every other word" Jerry Rubin used was an obscenity, but she couldn't bring herself to repeat the words. Pressed by Mr. Kunstler, all she would say was: "Every other word was that 'f' word."

"Haven't you ever heard that word in the station house?" Mr. Kunstler asked. Mrs. Callender looked embarrassed, the government objected and Judge Hoffman upheld the objection.

Ten days later, Mr. Kunstler got William Hale, a burly Chicago policeman, to concede he had used profanity to a TV cameraman in Grant Park. "I told him to turn those censored cameras around because of that civilian brutality," he said.

"What did you say when you said 'censored'?" Mr. Kunstler asked.

"There are ladies present," Mr. Hale replied. ". . . I will tell it to you or the judge, but—"

"In any event, it is immaterial," Mr. Foran broke in conveniently.

• • •

The government never seemed quite clear what the defendants' obscenity proved. When Mr. Schultz talked about Yippie "plans" for public fornication in Lincoln Park, he seemed bent on showing that the demonstrators were all heterosexual sex fiends and rapists.

29

But when Mr. Foran cross-examined Allen Ginsberg, he zeroed in on the homosexual themes in his poetry. The gentle poet's testimony provided one of the trial's most bizarre episodes, highlighted by his chanting of hindu mantras and Om-ing in court. But he also explained why he supported the Yippies' "fesival of life" during the convention: "The planet Earth at the present moment was endangered by violence, over-population, pollution, ecological destruction brought about by our own greed; that the younger children in America and other countries of the world might not survive the next thirty years; that it was a planetary crisis not recognized by any government of the world."

The morning before Ginsberg's second day on the stand, the owner of Barbara's Book Store in Chicago's Old Town section arrived to find a middle-aged man pacing up and down in front of the store. "Do you have any of Allen Ginsberg's books?" he asked. She went to look for them, but soon the man came over and said, "Could you hurry up? The future of the country may depend on this."

A few hours later, the books were on the table in front of Mr. Foran, and they formed the sole basis of his cross-examination. He asked Mr. Ginsberg to read several carefully selected poems, among them "Night Apple":

> Last night I dreamed
> Of one I loved
> Of seven long years,
> But I saw no face
> Only the familiar
> Presence of the body:
> Sweet skin eyes
> Feces urine and sperm
> Saliva all one
> Odor and mortal taste.

abbie

"Can you explain the religious significance of that?" the U.S. Attorney asked, his voice dripping with sarcasm.

"Well, if you could take a wet dream as a religious experience, I could," the poet replied.

As Mr. Ginsberg left the stand, several defendants overheard Mr. Foran sneer, "Damn fag."

At the time, I couldn't quite believe that; but after the trial Mr. Foran made his charge explicitly and more broadly. Contending that all of the defendants except Bobby Seale were "fags," he told the Loyola Academy Boosters Club, "We've lost our kids to the freaking fag revolution."

• • •

THE COURT: There comes a time when courtroom decorum must be observed.

MR. DELLINGER: Decorum is more important than justice, I suppose.

• • •

Unorthodox grooming and disregard for courtroom protocol is not disruption. And, contrary to the general impression, I don't believe there was ever a concerted, premeditated defense plan to disrupt the court. Sometimes the defendants themselves said things which suggested there was. ("We came here in August 1968 to disrupt the ritual and sham which is ordinarily put over as the democratic process," Rennie Davis wrote late in the trial. "Now we are disrupting the ritual and sham which Judge Hoffman calls the judicial process.") But such explanations strike me as ex post facto attempts to give the defense camp more order and cohesion than it ever had.

32

In fact, there was no single "defense strategy" and, given the differences in style and temperament among the defendants, there could hardly have been one. Those who attended some of the interminable defense meetings say the arguments about strategy and court-room demeanor often grew fierce.

The sharpest split—going back before the convention—was between the Mobilization Committee (Hayden, Davis and Dellinger) and the Yippies (Hoffman and Rubin). At the convention, the "Mobe" people wanted large, disciplined demonstrations focusing on the war and racism. The Yippies wanted a freer, more festive occasion in which people affirmed a "counter life style" and learned to "live the revolution." During the convention, each group was able to do its own thing; but seated around the same table, the differences sharpened.

Some defendants wanted to concentrate on winning the case in the courtroom, which meant a relatively straight, legal defense and some respect for courtroom protocol. Others were more concerned with persuading "the jury of the American people," which meant emphasizing the political aspects of the case and keeping the press interested with lots of flamboyant, unorthodox behavior. By and large, Tom Hayden took the most cautious line and Jerry Rubin the most flamboyant—with the others strung out between them, depending on time or circumstances.

But even had they agreed on a consistent, long-term strategy, they probably couldn't have carried it out. For the irreconcilable elements gathered in that courtroom were so volatile they had a self-generating logic of their own. Much of the time, the defendants could only respond to events—or exploit them—as imaginatively as possible.

One should remember that before the defendants

committed any of their 175 "contemptuous" acts, the judge took a step which many lawyers considered extraordinary. On the very first day of the trial, he ordered the arrest of four defense attorneys who failed to show up in court (the defendants had retained them to prepare pretrial motions and had not expected them to appear in court). Lawyers from all over the country came to Chicago to protest the judge's step; 126 of them filed an amici curiae brief terming his actions "a travesty of justice [which] threatens to destroy the confidence of the American people in the entire judicial process"; thirteen members of the Harvard Law School faculty asked the Senate Judiciary Committee to investigate the judge's conduct.

Moreover, it ought to be stated clearly that the defendants' contempt when it began was almost exclusively verbal. (No other aspect of the trial aroused such widespread confusion. Afterwards, a friend asked me which of the defendants had defecated in the aisle; I assured him none of them had.) The judge spoke several times of the defendants' "violence" in the courtroom. The only violence I witnessed occurred on several occasions when the federal marshals used more than necessary force to seat or lead away defendants (the defendants responded in kind, interposing a shoulder or hip between the marshals and their prey, but they did not attack anyone). The only other physical "actions" I recall were theatrical or symbolic: the attempt to bring a birthday cake into the courtroom on Bobby Seale's birthday; the placing of the National Liberation Front and American flags on the defense table, the wearing of judicial robes (unless you include the nonaction of refusing to stand). The rest of the time the contempt was words—irreverent, disrespectful, harsh and even vulgar—but words.

Finally, as Professor Harry Kalven of the University

of Chicago has pointed out, even this verbal contempt (as reflected in the contempt citations) was by no means consistent throughout the trial. It tended to bunch in periods of particular tension or confrontation, triggered by specific events. Other periods were largely calm, even tedious. Roughly, one could divide the trial into five phases:

Phase One—or "Jellybeans" as the defendants called it—lasted from the trial's start on September 24 through October 13. During that period, the defendants took a gently mocking stance toward the trial, symbolized by their distribution of jellybeans to the press and spectators. It was so uneventful that the judge found only six contempts during the three weeks —one of them Abbie blowing a kiss to the jury.

Phase Two—which I suppose could be called "Gags and Shackles"—lasted from October 14 through November 5. Some of the increased tension during this period may have stemmed from the defendants' feeling that their mockery had misfired and too many potential sympathizers regarded the trial as a joke. (As Abbie put it: "This trial is a comedy right down to the last day and then it'll be a tragedy.") Thus, the October 15 attempt to read a list of war dead was clearly an effort to emphasize the serious political issues implicit in the trial. But most of the contempts stemmed directly from Bobby Seale's continuing demand that he either be permitted counsel of his choice or the right to defend himself. The counsel of his choice was Charles R. Garry, a white Californian who had defended many Black Panthers and won their respect. But in August, Mr. Garry came down with a gall bladder condition which his doctors said required an immediate operation, and the defense asked a two-month postponement of the trial to permit him to recover. Judge Hoffman refused. When Seale was

35

brought here from California and held in Cook County Jail, Kunstler signed an "appearance" (normally signifying an intention to represent a client) so he could get in to see him. On September 26, when Seale rose to insist he was being denied his constitutional right to counsel, the judge seized on the appearance as evidence that he was adequately represented by Kunstler. And so the two antagonists were locked into position for an increasingly bitter conflict, which resulted in Seale being bound and gagged on October 29 and then on November 5 severed from the case, convicted on sixteen counts of contempt and sentenced to four years in prison. Unquestionably, he was in contempt much of the time. He flatly defied the judge on many occasions; and the epithets he flung about—"fascist dog," "racist," "pig," "rotten, low-life son of a bitch"—have rarely been heard in an American courtroom. I confess there were times when the empty clang of that rhetoric dismayed me. But his interjections were not random disruptions of the trial. By and large, he spoke only when it would have been proper for his attorney to speak in his behalf; his message, however phrased, was usually an appeal for his constitutional rights; and his language was often perfectly apt (Judge Hoffman: "You are making it very difficult for me, Mr. Seale"; Seale: "You are making it difficult for me, Judge Hoffman."). And whatever technical points the judge could find to buttress his position, the right to be represented by a lawyer you trust or, alternatively, to speak in your own behalf seemed to me so fundamental that I came to admire Seale's dogged persistence in its behalf. Moreover, one must recognize the pressures of guilt and revolutionary brotherhood which would not let the other defendants sit idly by while a black man was shackled and then hustled off to jail. In that context, the burst of contempts during this phase—fifty-four from October 28 to October 30 alone—is perhaps understandable if not forgivable.

Phase Three—call it "The Government's Day in Court"—lasted from November 6 until December 10 when the defense began its case. As Professor Kalven notes, there were only nine contempt citations during this period. This reflected in part natural decompression after the pressure cooker tensions of the Seale period; probably an element of caution once the judge had shown how tough he could be; and perhaps a growing recognition of just how weak the government's case was and a feeling that if they "cooled it" they just might squeak through with a hung jury.

Phase Four—"Sing Along with Phil and Judy"—was the early portion of the defense case, from December 11 to January 22. After a lengthy wrangle about whether to present a defense at all (some defendants felt they already had a hung jury and could gain nothing more), they decided to put on an elaborate political-cultural defense aimed largely at the "big jury out there." The defendants sought to explain and demonstrate their "identity"—through witnesses like Timothy Leary, the high priest of the drug culture and Jacques Levy, director of *Oh! Calcutta!* as well as through the songs of Phil Ochs, Judy Collins, Arlo Guthrie, "Country Joe" McDonald and Pete Seeger. There were relatively few contempts during this period, many of them growing out of arguments about the admissibility of such evidence.

Phase Five—"The Barnyard Epithet"—lasted from January 23 to February 7 when testimony was completed. This was a time of gradually building tension, culminating in the Epithet and the revocation of Dellinger's bail. The judge was massively overreacting now, often impulsively and even irrationally. Convinced they had him on the verge of some apocalyptic step, Abbie and Jerry shrugged off all restraints and cut loose with a barrage of grotesque Yippie raillery ("You're a disgrace to the Jews, runt," "Tell him to stick it up his bowling ball," "Mies van der Rohe was a Kraut too"). This period produced a cluster of forty-eight contempts.

• • •

TOM HAYDEN: . . . So, Your Honor, before your eyes you see the most vital ingredient of your system collapsing, because the system does not hold together.

THE COURT: Oh, don't be so pessimistic. Our system isn't collapsing. Fellows as smart as you could do awfully well under the system. I am not trying to convert you, mind you.

ABBIE HOFFMAN: We don't want a place in the regiment, Julie.

• • •

Through it all, Judge Hoffman looked down from his bench with an air of professorial distaste. At times, he reminded me of a spinster schoolteacher in a classroom of unruly children, forever rapping his ruler for order and sending children to stand in the corner, but stirring more trouble with each new act of discipline.

There were those around the courthouse who attributed the judge's snappishness to his height—barely 5 feet 4½ inches. Indeed, there was a small man's *machismo*, a feisty defiance, about the man. One of his favorite phrases—hurled repeatedly at the defense

39

attorneys—**was**, "You'll learn I don't frighten very easily."

Others said he was a bit of a snob. A confessed Anglophile, he has a leather-tooled Chippendale desk in his chambers and the walls are covered with engravings of English jurists—Lord Hardwicke, Lord Thurlow and Lord Ellenborough. When asked where he travels, the judge said, "Unlike Mr. Justice Douglas, we don't clamber around the Himalayas. I prefer London and the British Isles." When Mr. Kunstler remarked that some of the judge's friends probably used the word "hell" occasionally, he snapped, "I don't think you know any of my friends. . . . If they know you, they haven't told me about it." (At which Abbie, on the witness stand, murmured, "I know your chauffeur.") And when Mr. Kunstler referred to his residence, the spiffy Drake Towers, as "an apartment hotel," the judge flew into a rage, insisting it wasn't.

Others pointed to his age—seventy-four—which did seem to put him out of touch with even orthodox young people. While questioning one prospective juror, whose sister worked for Volunteers in Service to America (VISTA), he indicated he didn't know what the organization was. And when Country Joe of Country Joe and the Fish took the stand, the judge said—almost with pride—"I've never heard of him."

● ● ●

THE COURT: . . . I was a member of the faculty of the school that you—

LEE WEINER: I even understand that there is a plaque naming an auditorium after you at the Law School. At latest report, by the way—

THE COURT: You are nice to tell the assembled spectators here—

40

MR. WEINER: I tell them actually for an evil reason.

THE COURT:—that there is a Hoffman Hall on Northwestern University's campus.

MR. WEINER: I am telling them actually because I am suggesting it is evil.

THE COURT: Perhaps those who think ill of me because of some of the things that have been said might have a little compassion.

MR. WEINER: I am pleased to report to you that the plaque has been ripped off the wall.

THE COURT: The plaque?

MR. WEINER: Apparently while the Board of Trustees feels affection for you, the student body does not.

THE COURT: Did they take the sign off the door?

• • •

Others thought the judge was a pure ham, an egoist who thrived on the reactions he could draw from the other actors below him in the court and the spectators beyond.

The first week of the trial, Mr. Kunstler accused him of reading the indictment to the jury "like Orson Welles reading the Declaration of Independence." Feigning indignation, but obviously delighted, the judge said this was the first time in twenty-two years on the state and federal bench that anybody had complained about his voice. "I do my best to use the vocal facilities the Lord has endowed me with," he said.

And those facilities were remarkable. Orson Welles was only one of his many voices. Outraged, he was Lee J. Cobb; garrulous, Lionel Barrymore; insinuating, Vincent Price; cocky, Jimmy Cagney; grandfatherly, pure Edmund Gwenn.

At first, there was something almost endearing

41

about all this. The defendants nicknamed the judge "Mr. Magoo" and thought of designating him "an honorary Yippie," for he was a perfect foil for the courtroom theater some of them were trying to stage.

Yet, as the trial wore on, I felt he was more than an eccentric old curmudgeon. I began to see a pattern in his vocal theatrics and lapses of memory.

Invariably his inflections helped to underline a government point or ridicule the defense—and best of all, they would never show up in the stenographic appellate record. When he asked the court reporter to repeat a word, it was usually something like "erotic" or "vomit," whose emphasis could hardly help the defendants. He mispronounced Mr. Weinglass's name so often—as Weinstein, Weinberg, Feinstein, Fineglass, Weinrob, Weinramer or Weinruss—that it couldn't have been accidental. (Finally, at every fresh pronunciation, Abbie and Jerry took to holding up a cardboard sign spelling out in red Magic Marker: "Mr. Weinglass.") And his references to Mr. Kunstler as a "New York lawyer" were hardly designed to ingratiate him with a Midwestern jury. (As always, Abbie seemed to have an unerring sense for what his namesake was up to. Once when the judge remarked that Mr. Kunstler had practiced for years "in the Southern District of New York," Abbie added "when it was under British control.")

Perplexed by the judge's apparent partisanship, I sought out several Chicago lawyers who had practiced before him. They weren't at all surprised. Hoffman, they said, had long shown such a "blind spot for the government" that federal prosecutors often maneuvered to get their weak or sensitive cases before him. Federal court officials insist that case assignments are made by a "random selection" process involving tickets

torn off a pad. But lawyers here say it is well known that assignments can be juggled when the government wants a certain judge badly enough. Over the years Judge Hoffman has drawn a long list of sensitive cases —including the fraud trial of the men behind the anti-cancer drug, Krebiozen (which lasted nine months); the Stamler suit against the House Un-American Activities Committee; and cases against prominent syndicate gangsters like Anthony Accardo, William (Potatoes) Daddano, Sam (Teetz) Battaglia and Joseph (Joe Shine) Amabile.

The government won all these cases, and when the judge handed down his sentences he made it very plain he believed justice had been done. Sentencing gambler Tony Accardo to six years in prison for tax evasion, he denounced professional gambling as "a malignancy and a national catastrophe." When John Mirallegro was convicted of failing to pay the $50-a-year federal gambling tax, the judge imposed the maximum sentence of two years in prison and a $5,000 fine, noting "I'm getting a little annoyed with these gamblers taking up the court's time and the U.S. Attorney's time." And when he sentenced oft-convicted José Soto to twenty years in prison for selling heroin he said: "This man is a chronic criminal. There is no question of rehabilitation here. All we can do is take him out of circulation." This prompted the Chicago *American* to declare: "Hoffman is the bane of do-gooders who would give every bum a second chance, and a third and a fourth and a fifth."

He could also be tough on lawyers who vigorously defended such men. In 1952, while still on the state bench, he denounced lawyers who "manipulate witnesses and juries by means of strange courtroom antics and sensationalism." After sentencing Tony

44

Accardo, he accused two of the defense attorneys of "insolence, open defiance and vicious tactics." In 1966, he fined Chauncey Eskridge, a noted civil rights attorney, $100 for being thirty-five minutes late for a court date.

"So you see," one Chicago lawyer told me, "none of what he's doing now is all that new, and it doesn't have too much to do with his attitude toward the radicals. Julius has always regarded himself as the embodiment of everything federal. He sees the defense in any criminal case as the enemy, and he thinks it's his duty to help put them away."

• • •

One Saturday afternoon just before the trial began, Judge Hoffman was summoned from his home to hear an emergency defense motion.

When he mounted the bench, he saw before him not one of the defense attorneys but a young man in faded jeans and work shirt with a long reddish beard.

The young man said he was Stuart Ball, a June law school graduate not yet licensed to practice in Illinois but awaiting the results of his Washington, D.C., bar exam. He explained that he was there merely to file the motion on behalf of Mr. Kunstler, who was out of town.

"I will hear what you have to say," the judge said, "not as a lawyer but as a human being."

But as Mr. Ball briefly explained the motion—to permit Fred Hampton, the Illinois Black Panther leader (later killed by police in a raid), to visit Bobby Seale in prison—the judge grew increasingly angry.

He accused Mr. Ball of forging Mr. Kunstler's signature on the motion. And he ordered the Assistant

United States Attorney "to investigate the activities of this man Ball for coming into the United States District Court, getting a judge here from his home and without a license to practice law."

Then, turning to the young man, he asked, "Are you Stuart Ball's son?" (Stuart Scoble Ball, Sr., former president of Montgomery Ward and a partner in Sidley, Austin, Burgess and Smith, is one of the leaders of the Illinois bar.)

"Yes, Your Honor, I am," Stuart, Jr., replied.

"Well, you don't do credit to your father, sir," the judge said. "I am amazed. I have known your father for a long time. I consider him a professional and personal friend. He would not approve of your coming in here in this manner."

When I sought out Stuart, Sr., later, he declined to comment directly on the judge's remarks. But he said, "Everything my son has done in this case he has done after counseling with me. There has been no act of conduct on his part of which I am ashamed."

• • •

The judge can be a charmer with the ladies. (When an attractive blond lawyer appeared before him one morning, the judge set her trial date and then asked, "Are you sure you'll be in shape by then?" adding with a little smile, "I don't mean that literally.") He is an engaging dinner partner and an affable party-goer at some of Chicago's choicest affairs. That fall—with many young people waiting half the night outside the Federal Building to get a seat—the judge was in particular demand from hostesses eager for a pass to the jammed courtroom.

In early October, at least four of these ladies were

lee weiner

seen in the courtroom: Mrs. Bernard F. Rogers III, widely known as "Bumpy," who runs a chic boutique called Lencia on the Near North Side; Mrs. Henry D. Paschen, the former Maria Tallchief, who danced for years as the prima ballerina of the New York City Ballet; Mrs. Daniel J. Edelman, whose husband runs one of the country's ten largest public relations companies, and Mrs. James Goff, who in 1967 was a candidate for the international best-dressed list.

Mrs. Goff sat in the press section for more than a week. When I asked her whom she wrote for, she said she was a "free lance" and had gotten her pass "through friends."

Mrs. Rogers, Mrs. Paschen and Mrs. Edelman showed up together one morning. Later, Mrs. Rogers explained: "Oh, Ruth Edelman's a great friend of the judge's, you know. So we just went in and had a little chat with him—all three of us back in his chambers. He was so nice. He called a federal marshal and told him to take us into court."

The next day, five Negroes sporting bushy Afro hairdos took seats in the last row of the press section, reserved for the defendants' families. Judge Hoffman spotted the group, summoned the federal marshal who sat beside him and motioned toward the rear of the courtroom. The marshal quickly strode back and, with the help of assistants, removed the five.

When Mr. Kunstler rose to explain that they were Bobby Seale's wife and other relatives, Judge Hoffman curtly refused to hear him. "I leave seating in the courtroom completely to the marshals," he said.

• • •

Nothing irritated the judge more than charges that he was a racist. The charge struck me as just a mite too easy—the first radical reflex these days when a black is involved. True, the judge's handling of Mr. Seale seemed insensitive and vindictive, but he proved later in the trial that his vindictiveness knew no racial bounds.

Whenever the charge was raised, Judge Hoffman referred with obvious pride to his decision in the 1968 South Holland School case, the first court order for desegregation of a Northern school district. Yet somehow his declarations on the subject always seemed to come out of a different era—perhaps 1954, when he told a lawyer: "If there's any judge on the bench who looks after underprivileged members of other races, it's me."

In this trial, he was fond of telling defense attorneys that he was "the best friend" the Negro people had on the bench here. When a prospective juror mentioned that she once worked for Mr. Foran, the judge asked, "As a domestic?" No, she said, as a legal secretary. Another black juror said she was a cook. The judge seemed pleased. "Good cooks are hard to find," he said. When Dick Gregory took the stand for the defense, the judge positively beamed. "I would want this very nice witness to know . . . that he has made me laugh often and heartily." But when Mr. Kunstler said he could not direct Mr. Seale because he was "a free, independent black man who does his own direction," the judge said, "What an extraordinary statement, 'an independent black man' . . . he will be calling you a racist before you are through, Mr. Kunstler."

• • •

The judge, a German Jew, seemed equally testy about overt declarations of Jewishness. A young Orthodox Jew, wearing a yarmulke, tried repeatedly to get into the trial, but the federal marshals turned him away. Mr. Kunstler took the issue to the judge, who repeatedly refused to intervene.

Always quick to exploit such opportunities, the defense managed to get Arthur I. Waskow, a radical historian from the Institute for Policy Studies, on the witness stand wearing a yarmulke, and the following colloquy ensued:

THE COURT: Are you a clergyman, sir?
MR. WASKOW: No, sir.
THE COURT: You will have to remove your hat.
MR. SCHULTZ: Your Honor, we don't object. I know that he—
THE COURT: I object . . .

Shuddering with anger, the judge repeatedly ordered Mr. Waskow to remove his yarmulke or get off the stand—relenting only at Mr. Schultz's repeated urgings.

Sensing a vulnerability here, Abbie Hoffman responded one day by yelling at the judge in Yiddish: "Shonda fur de goyim" (which he gleefully translated as "front man for the WASP power elite").

That seemed a bit gross at first. But later I came to wonder whether the judge's efforts to escape his own Jewishness might not explain some of what went on in that courtroom. A man eager for social acceptance among the *goyim* might be gently condescending to *shvartses* like Mr. Seale, but his real rage would be reserved for the Jews who misbehaved (Messrs. Kunstler, Weinglass, Rubin, Hoffman and Weiner), and perhaps most of all for a thoroughgoing WASP like Mr. Dellinger, who had the social advan-

50

tages the judge craved but had given them up to join the Movement.

• • •

On February 9, members of the Radical Jewish Union attempted to exorcise the "dybbuk" which they claimed had possessed Judge Hoffman. The Union said the dybbuk—a wandering, demonic spirit—was that of Pontius Pilate who had possessed many souls over the past two thousand years, the last being Jeffreys of Wem, a chief justice under James II of England, who condemned more than three hundred persons to death.

In the shadow of the federal courthouse in New York's Foley Square, as several hundred lawyers, stenographers and passers-by looked on, eighteen of the Union's members, wearing white shrouds and prayer shawls, formed a circle to the blast of the ram's horn. They chanted a forty-minute liturgy, beginning:

> Wherefore, wherefore
> Did the soul from its
>   exalted height
> Fall into its abysmal
>   depth and
> Invade the body of this
>   wretched man
> To pervert justice and
>   negate life?

The Union said that while the dybbuk was being expelled, the judge might show pallor, irritability and spastic motions. During the time the ceremony was scheduled I watched the judge closely. He never looked better.

• • •

After Stalin's death in the early fifties, Western correspondents in Moscow used to gauge shifts in the Kremlin's power structure by watching the line-up of Soviet leaders atop Lenin's tomb. If Molotov moved one slot closer to Malenkov the press corps buzzed with excitement. If Beria turned his back on Khrushchev the correspondents nodded meaningfully. And back home, those meager scraps helped form foreign policy.

I often felt like a Kremlinologist as I scrutinized the jury for a hint of its reactions. Somehow the two long lines of jurors above the broad slab of the jury box reminded me of those pictures from Red Square. The jurors always sat in their assigned seats, but there were plenty of other subtle changes to give newsmen meat for speculation. During recesses and lunch hours we eagerly traded these bits of intelligence: Did you see that juror smiling at Abbie this morning? Did you see those two jurors whispering after the judge's ruling? Did that juror look bored or just tired? The defendants and their lawyers played the game even more assiduously, framing their strategy according to their assessment of the latest jury line-up.

After watching them for just a few days, nearly everybody on the press benches agreed the government could count on at least five of the jurors: Edward F. Kratzke, a florid-faced bus cleaner for the Chicago Transit Authority; John Nelson, an unemployed house painter who lived at a flop house on Chicago's skid row; Mrs. Miriam Hill, the night manager of a cafeteria, with a son in the navy, whose implacable scowl behind her bejewelled sunglasses soon earned her the nickname of "Mrs. Wallace" (after the Alabama governor); Mrs. Ruth L. Petersen, a graying housewife who recoiled noticeably when obscenities were uttered in the courtroom; and Mrs. Mildred Burns, a lady with pursed lips who rarely even looked at the defendants.

Two others were generally regarded as leaning toward the government: Mrs. Lorraine Bernacki, a stern-looking housewife married to a home rebuilder; and Mrs. Evelyn Hill, a light-skinned Negro who dyed her hair red.

This left five jurors with whom the defense thought it might have even a slim chance: Mrs. Mary Butler, a plump black woman with a warm smile; Mrs. Shirley Seaholm, a widow who followed proceedings in the courtroom with close attention; Mrs. Frieda Robbins, a small, birdlike divorcee with lively eyes and a thirty-one-year-old unmarried son who worked as an interior decorator; Miss Kristi King, at twenty-three by far the youngest member of the jury; and Mrs. Jean Fritz, a well-dressed suburbanite with two children in college who was seen carrying a James Baldwin book into the courtroom the first day, inevitably earning her the nickname "Mrs. Baldwin."

But within a week, one of those five was gone. After threatening notes ("You are being watched—The Black Panthers") were delivered to Miss King's and Mrs. Petersen's homes, the judge called both jurors in singly to ask whether they could still be impartial. Mrs. Petersen, who brought her letter to a federal marshal, said she had not been affected. But when Miss King came in, the judge instructed a marshal to hand her the letter and then asked whether she had seen it before.

"No," she said in a small, frightened voice.

"Has any member of your family ever brought it to your attention?" the judge asked.

"No, sir," she said, apparently close to tears.

"Having now seen it, will you please tell me if you can still be a fair and impartial juror in this trial?" the judge asked.

"No, sir, I cannot," Miss King replied.

With that, Judge Hoffman removed Kristi King from the jury and replaced her with the first alternate, a twenty-three-year-old computer operator named Kay Richards. The defense protested vigorously, arguing that the judge himself had "tainted" Miss King by showing her the letter. But the defendants were not overly disturbed because Miss Richards was also a young woman and presumed to be as open-minded as Miss King.

But as the trial wore on, the Kay Richards for Kristi King swap began to seem more important. Miss Richards sat next to Jean Fritz, and the two often whispered with each other or exchanged meaningful looks. Since Mrs. Fritz by then was generally regarded as the juror most favorably disposed to the defense, this led many people to assume that Kay Richards was also in the defense camp. But others thought they detected a cool, calculating look behind the prim little computer operator's glasses. And Tom Foran, a seasoned veteran at sizing up juries, told one reporter that Kay was "solid as a rock" for the government. Nobody knew until later just how solid she was.

• • •

The first defense witness permitted to testify was James M. Hunt, assistant safety supervisor at a Curtiss Candy Company plant and an amateur photographer who was present at the clash between demonstrators and police in Grant Park.

He introduced slides he took of the incident and testified that he saw police "chop" their way through the crowd, beating people on the head, knocking them down and kicking them. He said the police assault was "without provocation."

The next day, Mr. Hunt was fired from his job at Curtiss. Mark Woodward, director of industrial relations at the plant, said his discharge was unrelated to his testimony at the trial.

• • •

Every time the defense brought a new witness to the stand, Mr. Stanley, the F.B.I. man, would go through a strange ritual. After listening to a few minutes of examination, he would lean back, yawn, stretch and then rise and amble—oh so casually— toward the door. A few minutes later, he would reappear carrying a manila folder under his arm. Taking his seat, he would place the folder in front of him and then slowly nudge it across the table to Mr. Foran, who would begin scrutinizing its contents. It didn't take the defendants long to realize what Mr. Stanley was up to. Soon every time he rose to go, Abbie and Jerry would follow him with their outstretched fingers all the way down the aisle.

• • •

The antisubversives unit of the Chicago Police Department—known popularly as the Red Squad—has become something of a legend on the shores of Lake Michigan. Formed in the late nineteen-twenties to watch labor unions, it shifted its attention after World War II to "Communist fronts" and more recently to civil rights activists, radicals and hippies. But, apparently, its brief is almost unlimited. Under questioning by Mr. Kunstler, Lieutenant Joseph Healy, the squad's chief, said his unit kept tabs on "any organization that could create problems for the city or country."

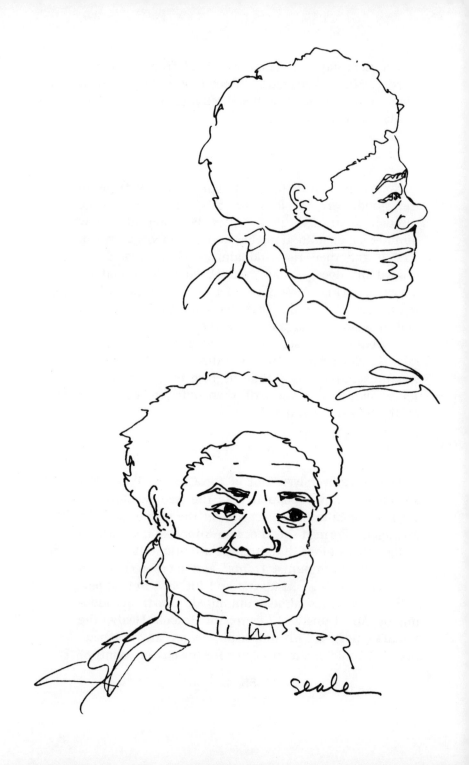

Now grown to more than forty men, the squad is divided into "overt" and "covert" sections. The overt agents, who snap pictures at meetings and demonstrations, are widely known to Chicago dissidents. At a recent press conference called by the Free Chicago Council, the chairman spotted a Red Squad man in the back of the room and announced: "Ladies and gentlemen, we'd like you to meet Morrie from the Red Squad." At demonstrations against the trial this winter, Red Squad men were easily identifiable in their canvas windbreakers, black turtlenecks, dark glasses—and cameras. As he passed them, Rennie Davis always waved and shouted: "Hi, fellas."

The covert section, on the other hand, positively revels in stealth. Until recently, it operated out of Mid-Continent Import-Export, a dummy corporation located on a pier in Lake Michigan. Groups of four undercover men report to "control officers" who alone are supposed to know their identities and missions—chiefly to infiltrate peace and radical groups.

Three of these men—Irwin Bock, William Frappolly and Robert Pierson—were the government's star witnesses. Bock, a young navy veteran who became active in Veterans for Peace, and Frappolly, who joined S.D.S. at Northeastern Illinois State College, both became demonstration "marshals" during the convention. Pierson, posing as a member of a motorcycle gang, became Jerry Rubin's "bodyguard."

Together they produced the heart of the government's case: that, while talking publicly about peaceful demonstrations, the defendants had actually plotted to take over downtown hotels, "sabotage" restrooms, firebomb an underground parking garage, stage a "mill-in" in the Loop, clog streets, pull fire alarms, break windows and, finally, "bust up the city" with "hit-and-run guerrilla tactics."

57

At times, as I listened, I was very nearly convinced. Their accounts were so smooth, so detailed, so coherent. They were nearly perfect witnesses. Perhaps just a shade too perfect.

For I was struck by how absurdly easy their jobs had been. They hadn't needed all the covert section's elaborate apparatus. They had volunteered their services to the demonstrators and had been accepted without screening. "Hell, we were accepting anybody in those days," Rennie Davis recalls. "We knew some of them were bound to be cops, but we didn't care. We didn't have anything to hide."

And I began to wonder, too, why the government hadn't found a single defector from the demonstrators' ranks. If the defendants had been so manipulative, if they had "used" idealistic McCarthy kids for their own violent purposes, why wasn't there at least one disillusioned kid willing to come forward and testify against them? Why this wholesale reliance on law-enforcement officials? The government's slate of witnesses included three city officials; four high-ranking police officers; five members of the Police Youth Division; six members of the Police Intelligence Division; two detectives; four special undercover agents; two undercover surveillance men; an F.B.I. agent; three paid informers; two military intelligence men; one Park District employee; a deputy sheriff; and (on rebuttal) six patrolmen. The only nonofficial witnesses called by the government were several newspapermen (most of them with close ties to the police), a cocktail waitress, a doctor and a young man just out of the navy.

• • •

"The Youth International Party cordially invites you

58

to attend the Fourth Annual Winter Dope Festival, to be held at the Chicago Museum of Science and Industry, at high noon on the Twentieth Day of December in the Year Nineteen Hundred and Sixty Nine. Black Tie Optional. B.Y.O.D."

Early in December, engraved invitations were handed out to spectators at the trial or posted in bars and bookstores around Chicago's Old Town section. So that Saturday, several hundred Chicago hippies, teeny-boppers and potheads showed up at the grandiose old museum on Lake Shore Drive. For more than an hour they sat on the cold stone steps waiting for Abbie, Jerry or any other Yippie to show up. None did. But the police came. Eight blue and white squad cars and two big squadrols lined up in the museum driveway, their grim-faced crews gazing apprehensively up the steps, ready for anything. Inside, Red Squad men and detectives tried to lounge casually around the lobby. Finally, after more than an hour, both sides realized they'd been had. The police roared off up the drive; the hippies pattered away across the park; and a few despondent curiosity-seekers drifted inside to watch steel balls jump through magnetic hoops or machines manufacture plastic busts of Abraham Lincoln.

• • •

The Yippies are the ultimate put-on artists. They have developed the practical joke and the April Fool's prank into finely honed political weapons.

One danger of relying on policemen for political intelligence is that they are notably literal-minded. And there is a theory that much of the violence in Chicago could have been avoided had the Red Squad—and its superiors—been better at sorting out foolery from ferocity.

Evidently, the police took quite seriously the Yippies' threat to put LSD in the city's water supply. Apparently, they were deeply concerned about "public fornication" in the park. One does not know how they reacted to announced plans to hijack the Chicago office of the National Biscuit Company to "provide bread and cookies for 50,000 young people." Perhaps they realized there is no office of the National Biscuit Company in Chicago.

The government contended that all these projects were part of the "Yippie myth"—a carefully designed effort to attract young people to Chicago and at the same time to frighten city officials into refusing permits for marches and sleeping in the parks. There is probably an element of truth in this. But, if so, Chicago goes right on falling for the Yippie myth.

On October 1, David Stahl, Mayor Daley's administrative assistant, testified about a meeting he had with Abbie Hoffman before the convention: "Mr. Hoffman said that if we, the city, were smart we would spend $100,000 to sponsor the 'festival of life,' or better yet, give him $100,000 and he would leave the city."

Under cross-examination, Mr. Stahl conceded he had told a Justice Department official that Mr. Hoffman "often spoke in jest." But he said he believed Mr. Hoffman's suggestion of a $100,000 bribe was "very serious."

Apparently, the Chicago *Tribune* had no doubt whatsoever. The next morning, a big, black, eight-column headline across its front page proclaimed: "Tell Yippie Cash Demand."

• • •

MR. SCHULTZ: Mr. Kunstler is laughing so he can influence the jury with the impression that this is absurd . . .

• • •

The judge was proud of his cutting wit and apparently enjoyed the laughter he could send rippling across the spectator section. But he was sensitive to any laughter coming from the defense table—particularly if he sensed it was directed at him. (He handed out several stiff contempt sentences—one of fifteen days—for laughing.)

Once, early in the trial, he admonished several jocular defendants to remain orderly, and Mr. Kunstler objected:

MR. KUNSTLER: Your Honor, a bit of laughter is not disorder, and I think sometimes—
THE COURT: It is in this courtroom. This is either a serious case or it isn't. I don't waste my time.

Once he even admonished Mr. Kunstler for smiling.

• • •

Nothing depressed me more during the trial than the legion of police informers whom the government paraded to the witness stand. I was astonished to find how easily ordinary Americans could be persuaded to spy on each other (there was a businessman from suburban New Jersey who got $10 plus expenses for attending Movement meetings and testified that he was recruited by a neighbor, an F.B.I. agent, while they watched a Little League baseball game).

But the informers who bothered me most were the

newsmen. I suppose our society will always need some undercover policemen. But it enraged me to see my profession used and subverted by the F.B.I. There was Carl Gilman, a cameraman for KFMB-TV in San Diego, California, who said he had been turning information over to federal agents since March 1968. There was Louis Salzman, a newspaper photographer who had become a fixture at radical gatherings in New York and even contributed pictures to Abbie Hoffman's book. He testified that he had been a paid informant for the F.B.I. since 1967. And, finally, several reporters from the Chicago *Tribune* and Chicago *Today* took the stand in the government's rebuttal case. While they were not informants, they had no hesitation about getting on the stand to corroborate police testimony.

I did not approve either of the Ohio newspaper editor and the Chicago newsman who testified for the defense. Partly as a result of this trial, I have come to feel that reporters simply do not belong on the witness stand in this kind of trial (perhaps in any kind of trial). Reporters have to cover both sides of this growingly polarized society, and I doubt that they can maintain a reputation for integrity and impartiality if they testify for either side.

• • •

Dragging through four and a half months, the trial had its dull stretches. So the twenty reporters regularly assigned to it devised some bizarre ways of passing the time. Mies van der Rohe's ceiling was one massive bank of fluorescent lights (prompting Abbie Hoffman to dub the courtroom "the neon oven"); and several newsmen soon calculated that the thin

63

steel partitions over the lights divided the ceiling into 56,576 tiny squares. One young lady (a child of the New Math, no doubt) spent an afternoon huddled over algebraic equations and announced that the diagonal was 342.51136 squares.

• • •

The jurors had it worst of all. After September 30, when the "Panther letters" were received, the jury was locked away in the Palmer House—virtually isolated from the world. Supervised twenty-four hours a day by federal marshals, they couldn't watch television, listen to the radio or read newspapers and magazines. But special entertainments were arranged. Every Friday and Saturday night, they had private showings of movies at the hotel: *South Pacific, Oklahoma! Music Man* and all the James Bond films.

And on December 26—as a special Christmas treat —they were taken to the "Disney on Parade" extravaganza at the Chicago Stadium: Mickey Mouse arriving in a giant balloon, a "Cinderella ball" with periwigged waltzers in satin gowns, a Dumbo circus with a chorus line of green, pink and white elephants, "go-go" monkey girls pulsating to rhythmic drums in a *Jungle Book* sequence and a madcap musical version of *Alice in Wonderland*.

• • •

The defendants spent most of their evenings speaking at colleges, women's clubs and churches to raise money for their defense. Although they anticipated a cold shoulder in "Pig City," as they called it, the reaction was often surprisingly warm and interested. One night, 1,400 people turned out to hear six of them speak at the Solel Congregation, a Jewish temple in Highland Park.

In Chicago's small, swinging liberal set, the defendants became instant celebrities and were invited to cocktail parties and dinners. One party took place last fall in an elegant townhouse on the Near North Side. Beginning rather sedately with a buffet dinner downstairs, it soon moved up to the second-floor parlor, where the defendants, their lawyers, staff and newsmen started dancing to Beatles and Rolling Stones albums. Before the night was over, Bill Kunstler had stripped off his shirt and Abbie Hoffman was down to his shorts.

But such bashes were relatively rare, in part because of the paranoia which affects so many Chicago "liberals." Several hostesses who contemplated parties for the defendants were persuaded they could damage their husbands' careers. When a group of ladies organized an art auction to benefit the Conspiracy late in the fall, several of them asked to have their names removed from the sponsors' list for fear of repercussions. A prominent businessman even refused to cash one defendant's check because he was worried about what his bank officials might think.

• • •

"Digger creed for meetings. Meetings are information, meditation, experience, fun, trust, rehearsals, drama. Meetings are not putting down people. Listen at meetings. Listen to eye movements. Listen to scratching. Listen to smells. Listen to great vibrations. Don't listen to words. . . . Beware of the structure freak. Beware of the rules. Beware of 'at the last meeting we decided.' Don't go back, there was no last

65

weinglass
weinruss
weinberg
weinraab
zwieglass
feinstein

meeting. Don't go forward. There is nothing."—Sign in the Conspiracy office.

• • •

The Conspiracy rented a suite of four rooms in an old office building at 28 East Jackson Street in the heart of the Loop. The "office"—if you could call it that —was soon covered with youth culture posters and ironic graffiti: "Karl Marx Was a Junkie," "We're Only in This for the Money," "Vietnam—Love It or Leave It," "Joe Hill Lives," "Get Big Brother First," "Remember What Happened to George III," and "Dave (red hair, black shirt) has been here a lot. He is on the Red Squad. Off You, Dave."

And just inside the big steel door was a mimeograph room with two particularly revealing signs: "This is the room where the slaves work," and "This is the corner where Dick works. He works here all day long. Work Dick Work. See Dick Work."

After the indictments came down, there was no shortage of volunteers for the Conspiracy staff. The defendants were the most glamorous, exciting leaders of the New Left, and their defense seemed to be where the action was in the Movement at that time. But the volunteers soon discovered most of that action was "shitwork"—typing letters, answering the phone, paying bills, making schedules, running mimeograph machines, carrying messages, arranging speeches, buying airline tickets.

Since the defendants had to spend five hours a day in court and many more hours in meetings, some staff members were often asked to provide even more personal services for them: taking their shirts to the laundry or buying them books and magazines. Some of the defendants, worried about the approaching verdict, became short-tempered and intolerant of work they considered less than efficient.

This was hard enough on the three or four male members of the staff. But it was particularly difficult for the ten women, most of whom were recent converts to Women's Liberation and began to resent deeply the defendants' "male chauvinism." In a taped discussion after the trial, printed in part by *Liberation* magazine, several of the staffers talked openly about their resentments. Elizabeth Langer complained, "The defendants were the stars and we were all working for them, putting them in the limelight. . . . I see it as a great tragedy. The Movement is not the defendants, and if they had been put in jail for ten years the Movement would go on without them." Susan Hathaway asked, "Am I working for Rennie Davis? No. I'm not sitting in that office because I want to help Rennie Davis in his life. . . . I'm working there because there is a place where I think I can get to people with the messages we have to give them. . . . And if I think that he is doing that wrong, why is it that he should have someone there to tell me to shut my mouth and type my letters?"

Several of the staff members did live with Tom Hayden and Len Weinglass in a big apartment in Hyde Park. There they tried to share domestic duties and privileges in the communal style now favored by many Movement people. Visitors to the commune might find women interviewing witnesses or sorting through files which filled rows of cardboard boxes in the bay-windowed living room, while some of the men whipped up a spaghetti dinner in the kitchen. But as tensions grew, the communal spirit waned. Before the trial was over, one of the women in the commune had quit the Conspiracy staff and joined the Weathermen (who are increasingly led by militant, independent-minded Weatherwomen).

• • •

THE COURT: What did you say about comparing a courtroom with a church, Mr. Witness? I am interested in that.

THE REVEREND RICHARD FERNANDEZ: I said you play more games in the courtroom than we do in a church.

THE COURT: I play games? Well, do you play games in a church?

REVEREND FERNANDEZ: Some people do.

THE COURT: They do? I didn't think clergymen did that of my faith.

REVEREND FERNANDEZ: Nor judges, I guess.

• • •

In one of its boldest ploys, the defense called Mayor Daley to the witness stand. From the start, it had maintained it would prove the defendants' innocence in part by showing who was really guilty of causing disorders during the convention. And the chief culprit, the defense contended, was Mayor Daley, who had conspired with his aides, police officers and some federal officials to stifle legitimate dissent and then halt demonstrations with clubs and tear gas.

Precisely because it feared questioning along these lines, the government had not called the mayor. This put the defense in a difficult position, for the open-ended, nonleading questions required in direct examination could not be expected to elicit much informa-

69

tion from the mayor. The only hope—a slim one—was to get the mayor declared a "hostile" witness, which would permit the defense to cross-examine him as though he were a government witness.

As expected, the judge refused. "Nothing in the mayor's behavior indicates that he is hostile," the judge said with a little smile. "His manner has been that of a gentleman." And so, surrounded by the protective judge, the solicitous U.S. Attorney and four vigilant bodyguards, the mayor sat patiently and almost silently through the long, futile examination. Mr. Kunstler would ask about the mayor's relationship with city officials; his April 15, 1968, order to "shoot to kill" arsonists; or his shouted remarks at Senator Abraham Ribicoff during the convention (which Mr. Kunstler, rushing quickly to get the words before the jury, said were, "Fuck you, you Jew son of a bitch, you lousy motherfucker, go home"). Mr. Foran would leap up and object to the leading question. Judge Hoffman would uphold the objection and warn Mr. Kunstler not to ask "another one like that."

•   •   •

(Just a month before, on November 12, the following colloquy took place:

MR. KUNSTLER: Your Honor, I object again. That is a leading question to tell him there was a meeting which he attended—

THE COURT: Mr. Kunstler, do a little research on this matter of leading questions. Really, evidence authorities are not very much against leading questions these days.)

70

• • •

The few questions Mr. Kunstler was allowed to ask Mayor Daley brought only the blandest of replies. Asked what instructions he had given city officials about how to handle the Yippies, the mayor said he had ordered that they be given "every courtesy and hospitality while they were in the city of Chicago."

After the noon recess, the mayor, watched closely by his bodyguards, returned to the courtroom early and took his seat in the witness box. Abbie Hoffman, seated alone at the witness table, turned and saw him. Rising slowly, he sauntered up the aisle toward the mayor and in his best Gary Cooper-*High Noon* drawl said, "Why don't we settle this here and now—just you and me? The hell with all these lawyers."

• • •

At times, I confess, I felt much the same way. For all too often the legal apparatus of the court seemed only to hinder the search for truth. Judge Hoffman is known as a first-class legal technician. But a judge has wide latitude in interpreting the rules of evidence, and most of Judge Hoffman's interpretations seemed to cut one way—for the government.

Many of them excluded evidence or witnesses which the defense considered important to its case. The most widely publicized exclusion involved Ramsey Clark, whom the judge barred from testifying before the jury (after he heard him examined out of the jury's presence and concluded that he could make "no relevant contribution" to the case). The ruling brought vehement protests from the defense ("absolutely unheard of in the history of the United States") and ringing condemnations from liberals outraged that the jury could not hear from the country's former chief legal officer, particularly one so intimately involved with security preparations for the Chicago convention.

Privately, however, some defendants conceded that Mr. Clark couldn't have added much legally admissible evidence. They—and many lawyers—were far more disturbed by the judge's exclusion of several documents written by the defendants themselves: two articles which Abbie Hoffman wrote for the underground press in the summer of 1968 describing plans for the "festival of life" and a long paper written by Rennie Davis and Tom Hayden in March 1968 on their strategy for Chicago.

The Davis-Hayden document, submitted to a conclave of radicals at Lake Villa, Illinois, said in part: "The campaign should not plan violence and disruption against the Democratic convention. It should be nonviolent and legal. The right to rebellion is hardly exercised in an effective way by assembling 300,000 people to charge into 30,000 paratroopers. In fact, any plan of deliberate disruption will drive away people who are worried about arrests or violence, and thus sharply diminish the size and political effect of the mobilization. Little would be served, except perhaps the political hopes of Johnson, Nixon and Wallace, by a Chicago action that would be seen (as Max Lerner sees it in his fantasy already) as a gathering of 'every crackpot group, protest group, every disruptive, violent force in American society that thinks it has a pipeline to the absolute truth.' We must demonstrate the opposite, that the government is the real source of crackpot thinking and violence."

This document was excluded as "self-serving." If it had proposed bomb-throwing or killing policemen the government could certainly have introduced it as proof of the charges in the indictment. But because it urged just the opposite it was deemed "self-serving" and inadmissible. How, I wondered, could a defendant prove his intent if he could not introduce evidence of that intent?

• • •

THE COURT: This is not a political case as far as I am concerned.

MR. KUNSTLER: Well, Your Honor, as far as some of the rest of us are concerned, it is quite a political case.

THE COURT: It is a criminal case. There is an indictment here. I have the indictment right up here. I can't go into politics here in this court.

MR. KUNSTLER: Your Honor, Jesus was accused criminally, too, and we understand really that was not truly a criminal case in the sense that it is just an ordinary—

THE COURT: I didn't live at that time. I don't know. Some people think I go back that far, but I really didn't.

MR. KUNSTLER: Well, I was assuming Your Honor had read of the incident.

• • •

Only Mr. Kunstler would have dared compare the trial with the crucifixion. But there were others who rankled at the judge's rigid interpretation of what the trial was all about.

Take Richard Goodwin, former aide to Presidents Kennedy and Johnson and campaign director for

Senator Eugene McCarthy in 1968. Mr. Goodwin was permitted to testify briefly about conversations he had had with Tom Hayden and David Dellinger before the convention. But the judge refused to let him answer questions about relations between demonstrators and Senator McCarthy's supporters.

Later at a news conference, Mr. Goodwin—a former editor of the *Harvard Law Review* and clerk to the late Justice Felix Frankfurter—took issue with the judge's rulings. "The rules of evidence are not graven in stone," he said. "There is a great deal of flexibility in them if one really wants to get at the truth. But the judge is interpreting them in such a fantastically restrictive way that it is very difficult to get to the truth." Had he been permitted to testify more freely, Mr. Goodwin said, he would have told the jury that none of the defendants had the power to bring about violence in the streets of Chicago. Most of the young people in the city during convention week were McCarthy supporters who owed no allegiance to the radicals. "If Rennie Davis and Tom Hayden stood in the middle of Michigan Avenue and yelled 'charge,' about five people would have followed them."

Or take Norman Mailer. From the start, it was plain that Mailer had come back to exorcise a nagging sense of guilt about his own role that week in Chicago. On the bandstand in Grant Park that Wednesday, he had told the crowd he couldn't take part in their demonstration because he had a magazine deadline to meet and couldn't risk getting arrested. The radicals didn't buy that, and some even suggested that the Champ was frightened. Ever sensitive about slights to his manhood, Mailer had brooded about the charge ever since and, on the witness stand, he tried to grapple

honestly with his own emotions: "I was in a moral quandary. I didn't know if I was being scared or being professional, and I was naturally quite upset because a man never likes to know that his motive might be simple fear."

But Judge Hoffman was impatient with all this motivational probing. "We're simple folks here," he snapped once. "Just tell us what you said and he said." Finally, as Mailer continued to search out delicate shadings of meaning in the streets of Chicago, Dick Schultz leaped up and told him to stick to "the facts." Mailer snapped back: "Facts are nothing without their nuance, sir."

Later, at a news conference, Mailer denounced the "ridiculously low level of yes and no questions" required at the trial. "This isn't an accident case. If you're trying people on a conspiracy charge, at least the defense ought to be entitled to go into an explanation of their political positions." If he had been permitted to testify more fully, Mailer said, he would have explained why he regarded the conspiracy charge as ridiculous: "Left-wingers are incapable of conspiring because they're all egomaniacs." Moreover, he said, the defendants had "understood that you don't have to attack the fortress anymore. You just surround it, make faces at the people inside and let them have nervous breakdowns and destroy themselves. That's an extraordinary conspiracy."

• • •

"He [Mr. Foran] says we are un-American," Abbie Hoffman noted when he addressed the court just before sentencing. "I don't feel un-American. I feel very American. . . . It is not that the Yippies hate America.

77

It is that they feel the American dream has been betrayed." Then pointing to the portraits of the Founding Fathers behind the bench, he went on: "I know those guys on the wall. I know them better than you, I feel. I know Adams. I mean I know all the Adamses. They grew up twenty miles from my home in Massachusetts. I played with Sam Adams on the Concord Bridge. I was there when Paul Revere rode right up on his motorcycle and said, 'The pigs are coming, the pigs are coming.' Right into Lexington."

● ● ●

Staughton Lynd, the radical American historian, was another defense witness whom Judge Hoffman would not let testify before the jury. When Mr. Weinglass said the defense wanted to qualify Professor Lynd as "an expert on the American Revolution," Mr. Foran leaped up to protest. "As to the American Revolution," he said, "there is no charge in the indictment about that." The judge upheld him.

The paper which Professor Lynd would have read the court argued that some of the things that happened in Chicago in 1968 were "remarkably similar to certain events of the period of the American Revolution"—particularly the Boston Massacre of March 1770, in which British soldiers fired into a crowd of colonists, killing five. "Each side blamed the other for what happened," Mr. Lynd wrote. "The British said that the soldiers had been surrounded in the middle of the night by a mob of angry townspeople who threw lumps of ice and oyster shells at the soldiers and screamed things like 'Come on you rascals, you bloody backs, you lobsters, scoundrels, fire if you dare.' (The term 'lobster' referred to the red uniform of the British regular. It was the eighteenth-century equivalent of 'pig.') To this the colonists, such as Sam Adams and Paul Revere . . . pointed out that in normal times the town of Boston had a police force of about ten men. Since October 1768, however, two to four regiments of British troops had been stationed in Boston because of the alleged rebelliousness of its people. Far from preventing disorder the troops were themselves a cause of it. . . . What to the British seemed a riot planned by scheming conspirators like Sam Adams, to Adams and his friends seemed a riot by the 'police.' "

But to Lynd the comparisons between 1770 and 1968 went deeper. "The government says the defendants conspired to cause a riot," he wrote. "I, on the contrary, say that they organized a process of petitioning just as Sam Adams and Tom Jefferson did before them. . . . American revolutionaries did not pass at once or in one step from peaceful petitioning to insurrection. As their petitions were rebuffed they experimented with a variety of tactics intermediate between customary speech-and-assembly, on the one hand, and, on the other, what John Locke called the 'appeal to heaven' of revolution. . . . I believe that this conceptual framework puts the relatively minor violence which took place here in Chicago in the right perspective. The people coming here were no longer content to ask favors. They believed the rights to assemble, to speak, to march to be rights not privileges, and when permission to exercise those rights was not forthcoming they exercised them anyway. . . . If as a people we believe that a severely oppressive government justifies revolution, how can we not believe that a partially undemocratic and oppressive government justifies acts of resistance short of revolution. If under circumstances we can kill kings, must there not be lesser circumstances in which we can say no to them?"

● ● ●

When Rennie Davis took the stand on January 23, he was carrying part of an American antipersonnel bomb he had been given in Hanoi.

THE COURT: The exhibit is wholly irrelevant and immaterial. If an exhibit like this were to be permitted, you could fill this room with bullets. I am not trying the Vietnamese war here. . . . There is no such charge in the indictment.

MR. WEINGLASS: Well, that goes to the question, Your Honor, of the relevance of the war as an issue in this trial. . . . Now, Mr. Davis, together with six others, is charged with coming to the city to incite a riot. That's the government's contention. Our contention is that they came to the city to demonstrate peacefully about two overriding social issues, the war and racism.

● ● ●

From the defendants' point of view, their most important witness was probably Linda Morse, the former pacifist and peace march organizer who admitted that she now practiced karate and fired her M-1 in preparation for the violent revolution she believed was inevitable. Tall and rather pretty in a severe way, with long, golden-blond hair streaming down her back, she obviously intrigued the predominantly female jury. As they watched her closely—some with perplexed sympathy, others with utter revulsion—they were clearly wondering how a young Quaker girl from Philadelphia (where she had won a Kiwanis Decency Award) could end up like this.

Her frank, unhesitating talk about violent revolution astonished many reporters, too. As we came out of the courtroom that afternoon, Rennie Davis walked over and asked, "What did you think of her?" One reporter said, "Well she was certainly a disaster for you. Now you've really had it." But clearly Rennie didn't agree. He and many of the other defendants were almost ebullient because, for the first time, a witness had been allowed to talk at length about the need for revolutionary change in America.

Much of what Miss Morse said on that subject probably would have been ruled out of order had it been elicited on direct examination by a defense attorney. It slipped in during cross-examination because Dick Schultz, obviously exultant at having bared Linda the Street Fighter, was rushing ahead to press his advantage. "One of the reasons further for your revolution is your opposition to capitalism and imperialism, isn't that right?" he asked, quoting from her interview in *Playboy*. Miss Morse said that was right. "And the more you realize our system is sick, the more you want to tear it limb from limb, isn't that right?"

But at that, Miss Morse launched into a long response which, in retrospect, seems the most coherent explanation offered during the entire trial of what at least some of the defendants' revolution is all about:

"The more that I see the horrors that are perpetuated by this government, the more that I read about things like troop trains full of nerve gas traveling across the country where one accident could wipe out thousands and thousands of people, the more that I

81

U.S. marshals

see things like companies just pouring waste into lakes and into rivers and just destroying them, the more I see things like the oil fields in the ocean off Santa Barbara where the Secretary of the Interior and the oil companies got together and agreed to continue producing oil from the off-shore oil fields and ruined a whole section of the coast, the more that I see things like an educational system which teaches black people and Puerto Rican people and Mexican-American people that they are only fit to be domestics and dish-washers, if that, the more I see a system that teaches middle-class whites like me to continue producing CBW warfare, to continue working on computers and things like that to learn how to control people better, yes, the more I want to see that system torn down and replaced by a totally different one—one that cares about people learning; that cares about children being fed breakfast before they go to school; one that cares about people going to college for free; one that cares about people living adult lives that are responsible, fulfilled adult lives, not just drudgery, day after day going to a job; one that gives people a chance to express themselves artistically and politically and re-ligiously and philosophically. That is the kind of sys-tem I want to see in its stead."

• • •

MR. KUNSTLER: . . . You know it is not right. To call a man "phony" and "two-faced" in oral argument is not right. We both know that. You don't say anything and you are countenancing the remark.

THE COURT: For your information, maybe you don't know it, the word "phony" is in the dictionary.

MR. KUNSTLER: So is the word "pig," Your Honor.

• • •

The two government attorneys made an effective pair, their courtroom styles contrasting but nicely complementing each other. While Schultz's objections rose in a soaring crescendo ("Your Honor, that's the most outrageous . . ."), Foran's trailed off in a sigh of weary disgust, which Kunstler called his "dying quail" gambit ("Oh, are you going through all that again?").

In two years as U.S. Attorney for the Northern District of Illinois, Tom Foran had won a reputation as a tough racket-buster. He packed off to prison dozens of Chicago's crime syndicate hoodlums; piled up an impressive courtroom record (202 wins and 33 losses); and boasted a close working relationship with the F.B.I. (At a testimonial dinner for Mr. Foran in June, Martin W. Johnson, the former head of the F.B.I.'s Chicago office, said, "I really love this man.")

But he had a liberal image, too. He was fond of stressing his friendship with former Attorney General "Bob" Kennedy, who he said was a "better friend" of his than of Tom Hayden's (who stood guard at Kennedy's funeral bier). And he sometimes invoked the imagery of the New Frontier: "The lights in that Camelot the kids believe in needn't go out. The banners can snap in the spring breeze. The parade will never be over if people will remember and go back to what Thomas Jefferson said: 'Obedience to the law is the major part of patriotism.' "

But as former Assistant Corporation Counsel for Chicago, he was even closer to Mayor Daley, who described Foran from the witness stand as "one of the greatest attorneys in this country and the finest man I have met in private and public life." Although many U.S. attorneys are closer to the local politicians who got them their jobs than they are to the Attorney General, Foran's loyalty to Daley was particularly emphatic. In April 1968, when Chicago was in flames following Martin Luther King's death, the mayor didn't want to admit he could not keep peace in his city. So Foran called Ramsey Clark for him to ask for federal troops (which he had no authority to do).

Foran has the stocky good looks of an Irish cop or a bantam-weight prizefighter, with a hard, compact body that looked as though it had been poured into his sharply creased gabardine suits. His steel-gray hair was always beautifully combed and his cherubic cheeks closely shaved, as if he had just spent a long time in a barber's chair.

For most of the trial, he was the government's straight man—composed, restrained, a professional doing a dirty job. His early jibes at Kunstler—"mouthpiece," "Perry Mason"—could be written off as a pro's reaction to amateurish grandstanding. In his summation to the jury he cut loose, denouncing the defendants as "evil men," "liars and obscene haters," "profligate extremists more concerned with their own needs than the common good." But not until the Boosters Club speech did he reveal the full anger he had kept bottled up all winter. Striding around Loyola's basketball court, giving limp-handed waves in describing defendants and members of the press, he denounced Abbie Hoffman as "scummy," David Dellinger as "a sneak who uses people like a ventriloquist," and Norman Mailer as "an utter jackass."

Dick Schultz, Mr. Foran's assistant, was a damp and awkward young man. He was also very bright and very ambitious. His mind had absorbed, catalogued

and cross-referenced every detail of the "Conspiracy," and he was able to pull any reference out at a moment's notice to brandish in front of the court and jury. It was an impressive feat; at times, he could even make the whole thing sound believable. But he had an incredibly literal mind, too. Everything had its place in the grand scheme; nothing was left to chance or spontaneity. "Nothing Mr. Kunstler does is involuntary," he said one day. Schultz could have made the first robin of spring sound like a plot by the Audubon Society.

From the start, he betrayed an instinct for the jugular. He sounded perpetually outraged. Listening to a bit of testimony or examination he didn't like, a red flush would creep across his neck and face, his thick lips would twist into a snarl and he would leap toward the lectern denouncing the defendants or their attorneys for some unspeakable new crime. The defendants soon labeled him a "tattletale" for his habit of rushing to the bench to report on what they had done while the judge was out of the courtroom. This habit led to one of the trial's worst uproars. Before court began on October 29, Bobby Seale addressed a group of Black Panthers in the spectator section. He told them it would be a lively day and warned them, "You be cool, here, you be cool." If they were attacked, he said, "you know the principles of the party. Defend yourselves." But when the judge came in a few minutes later, Schultz reported, "He was talking to those people about an attack by them."

• • •

MR. KUNSTLER: Your Honor, there is an old maxim in law that if the police are brutal to one group, there is an inference they may be brutal to other groups, and that is a—

THE COURT: That is a maxim of the law I never heard of, and I sustain the objection.

MR. KUNSTLER: You heard the maxim that "False in one thing, false in all?" That is what I am saying: "Falsus in uno, falsus in omnibus." That is the maxim.

THE COURT: You ought to put on your striped trousers and be a professor.

MR. KUNSTLER: Your Honor, I am afraid I don't have striped trousers.

THE COURT: I didn't ask you for a lecture. . . . I don't know all of those fancy phrases that you used.

• • •

After the two Hoffmans, Bill Kunstler was the most compelling figure in the courtroom. He drew the eye, whether sprawled in his rumpled suit at the defense table twirling his horn-rimmed glasses or standing tall and gaunt in the well of the court sparring with the judge. Some say he was "showboating" much of the time. Certainly he had an ego to match any in the courtroom. Once, he told the judge they had the same birthday (July 7). The judge asked how he'd found that out:

MR. KUNSTLER: I compared our Who's Who in *Who's Who in America* . . .

THE COURT: Very brief, wasn't it?

MR. KUNSTLER: No, yours was, I think, three lines shorter than mine.

Those few cramped lines in the big red book do reflect an extraordinary career: a striking if gradual transition from a conventional middle-class Jewish

88

upbringing in New York, Yale, Columbia Law School and the R. H. Macy executive training program, through family and small business law to civil libertarian and civil rights causes, and now a deepening immersion in the radicalism of the Movement.

That transition continued throughout the trial. Many people assume that the man who had represented Martin Luther King, Jr., Stokely Carmichael, H. Rap Brown, Adam Clayton Powell, Malcolm X and the Black Panthers came to Chicago a full-blown radical. But in September 1969 he was probably not much more than a flamboyant liberal (a year before he had voted for Hubert Humphrey). I remember one night in late September, just after the trial began, visiting him in the tiny apartment he had borrowed from a friend. Propped up on his bed, surrounded by stacks of briefs and pretrial motions, he talked of the "incredible tensions" in that courtroom. As I left, I remember him saying, "Well, it's going to be an education anyway. I learn something new from every case."

From this one, it seems, he learned how difficult it is to maintain the traditional "officer of the court" stance in an overtly political trial with clients like these. There are lawyers who say it can be done; that, in fact, if Kunstler had insisted on maintaining his separate identity and fighting with traditional legal tools he could have won this case. Perhaps. But that misses the central point: that for these defendants winning the case was not the first priority. If the courtroom becomes a political battleground as this one did, then a lawyer cannot stand in no man's land waving his arms and making objections. He must choose sides. Ultimately, not without some personal soul-searching, Kunstler did.

He let his hair grow longer and longer, until it

curled around his ears and flopped over the collar of his colored shirts. He ate with the defendants, drank with them, danced with them, demonstrated with them. On November 15, he joined the March Against Death, in Washington, and when he got back to Chicago, the judge asked him what he'd done. "I sang once and I listened to the speeches. I sat on top of a tractor trailer, and I was thrilled by what I saw as I looked out at what seemed to me half a million people who had one thought in mind, and that was to end the war in Vietnam." A few days later, the judge told him "you get awfully chummy with your clients"; and he replied "there is a certain intimacy that is bred in these cases."

That intimacy led him to some probably calculated bits of courtroom melodrama—crying "stop this medieval torture" during the restraining of Bobby Seale, or embracing Dr. Ralph Abernathy in front of the jury. But it also churned up powerful emotions. I have no doubt he was absolutely sincere when on February 2 he told the judge, "I am going to turn back to my seat with the realization that everything I have learned throughout my life has come to naught, that there is no meaning in this court, there is no law in this court"; or when on February 14, after the sentencing of Dave Dellinger, he broke into tears at the lectern, pleading, "Put me in jail now, for God's sake, and get me out of this place. Come to mine now. Come to mine now, Judge, please. Please. I beg you. Come to mine. Do me, too. I don't want to be out."

But even the lawyers who defend this kind of emotional involvement with a case make one telling criticism of Mr. Kunstler: he simply didn't work hard enough at the law. Thriving on the drama and excitement of courtroom confrontation, he was bored by long hours over books and briefs. Too often he was ill-prepared for an argument or a cross-examination. Nobody could "wing it" like Kunstler, but even in a case like this one winging it wasn't enough.

The workhorse of the defense was Lennie Weinglass. Night after night, he would rush through dinner and then spend hours meticulously preparing for the next day. Curiously, the judge singled him out at the start for his particular scorn, perhaps because he wore his hair long and dressed with a mod flair. Nick von Hoffman overheard the judge in the elevator saying, "Now we are going to hear this wild man Weinglass," but from then on he managed to mangle the name every time he spoke it and seemed to delight in curt little put-downs of the young lawyer ("I would like to preside over a class in evidence, but I haven't the time today").

But my respect for Len grew daily. He had a stolid decency which allowed him—alone among all the figures in that courtroom—to maintain a semblance of dignity throughout the trial. Clearly, he was torn by the conflicting demands on him: his obligations to the court, which he took more seriously than Kunstler; and his obligations to his clients, who became his close friends. He tried to balance these two duties as best he could, rarely resorting to theatrical stunts but often maintaining his right to continue a line of questioning after the judge had ordered him to stop. For his efforts he was sentenced to one year, eight months and three days in prison for contempt.

* * *

"PROSECUTOR: Ding dong dell. Daley's feeling swell. We've caught the little smarties who crashed last sum-

91

jacques levy

mer's parties. The F.B.I. would never lie. Just look and you can tell.

"JUDGE: That's enough. Jury, consider your verdict.

"PROSECUTOR: Not yet, not yet, there's a great deal more.

"DEFENSE LAWYER: Besides there's no jury.

"JUDGE: Overruled. Where is the jury? Mr. Clerk, if the jury is not here in half a minute ago, I shall have them executed on the spot."

This was part of a skit called "Alice in Wonderland" in the Chicago Bar Association's annual Christmas show. The next day, the sharp satire of Judge Hoffman was condemned in a ringing editorial by the Chicago *Tribune,* which termed it "a deplorable offense against good taste." Chief Judge Campbell chimed in, calling it "a clear violation of the canons of professional ethics." The association refused to delete the skit but in later performances added a section satirizing the defense attorneys.

• • •

The Queen of Hearts passed "sentence before the verdict." And sure enough, the moment the jury went out to begin its deliberations, Judge Hoffman began sentencing the defendants and their attorneys to lengthy prison terms for contempt of court.

He has been widely criticized for some of the individual sentences: six months to Dellinger for calling him "Mr. Hoffman" instead of "Your Honor"; four days to Abbie Hoffman for baring his rib cage in front of the jury; fourteen days for applauding; fifteen days for laughing; a month for refusing to sit down.

But the judge's sweeping use of his contempt power raises far larger questions. Can a judge get around the general lower court judgment that any penalty over six months requires a jury trial by dividing the contempt into individual crimes and passing sentences up to six months for each crime? Most lawyers with whom I have spoken feel this is a palpable evasion and will be so adjudged by the appeals court.

Should a judge be permitted to convict and sentence in a matter so involving his own emotions and ego? The late Justice Frankfurter, dissenting in *Sachar* v. *United States,* wrote: "The judge acted as the prosecuting witness; he thought of himself as such. His self-concern permeates the record; it could not humanly have been excluded from his judgment of contempt. . . . Precisely because a judge is human and, in common frailty or manliness, would interpret such conduct of lawyers as an attack on himself personally, he should not subsequently sit in judgment on his assailants, barring only instances where such extraordinary procedure is compellingly necessary in order that the trial may proceed and not be aborted."

More particularly, should a judge be able to punish the conduct of attorneys who practice before him? Justice Black, also dissenting in *Sachar,* wrote: "I cannot reconcile this summary blasting of legal careers with a fair system of justice. Such a procedure constitutes an overhanging menace to every courtroom advocate in America. The menace is most ominous for lawyers who are obscure, unpopular or defenders of unpopular persons or unorthodox causes."

• • •

MR. KUNSTLER: Is it your testimony, finally, Deputy, before this jury, that you were entirely satisfied with the performance of your policemen at the intersection of Michigan and Balbo between 7:45 P.M. and 8:15 on the evening of August 28?

DEPUTY SUPERINTENDENT OF POLICE JAMES M. ROCHFORD: I'm never satisfied.

MR. KUNSTLER: And could you indicate to the jury what your particular complaint about your police performance at the time was?

SUPERINTENDENT ROCHFORD: Well, my real concern —it's not a complaint. Each and every time we have a police operation, we examine it, we go to the very basic operating level and we ask for information and evaluation reports. I felt badly and was hurt that people were injured, that in this great city of Chicago this incident occurred in the manner that it did. I have concern for anyone injured. My basic responsibility is to protect life and property. But after reconsidering all the circumstances and all the information that I had at my fingertips, I could not be too critical of this operation.

• • •

We heard a lot of testimony from both sides about what happened in the streets of Chicago during the convention—particularly about what happened in Grant Park and on Michigan Avenue in front of the Conrad Hilton Hotel on August 28. The government said the demonstrators rioted. The defense said the police rioted. The government produced witnesses and films which it said proved that the demonstrators had charged into police ranks, throwing bags full of urine and spiked balls. The defense presented other witnesses and films which it said proved the police charged the demonstrators, swinging their clubs with wild abandon.

After a while I came to wonder just why we were

"Mrs. Wallace"

sitting through all this. From my own observations during convention week, I had a pretty clear idea about who had done what to whom. The police had reacted with disproportionate force to some provocation—largely verbal or symbolic—from the demonstrators. At worst, it seemed to me, some demonstrators might be guilty of "inciting a police riot." But, for purposes of this trial, none of that really seemed to matter. The defendants were not charged with rioting or even inciting a riot. If the cherubim and seraphim had danced up Michigan Avenue that week it wouldn't have affected the legal issue. What mattered, the prosecution kept telling us, was not what actually happened but what the defendants intended to happen.

When the conspiracy charge was coupled with the antiriot act, the legal issue was taken one step further from what happened in the streets. In effect, the defendants were charged with an intention to intend. But the government was unable to prove even that. By the prosecutors' own admission, the eight "conspirators" never met together as a single group before the convention. Bobby Seale had never met any of the others. And even with regard to the five main figures, the government never proved a common intent linking the Yippies and the Mobilization. Strangely, not a single word of testimony was offered during the government case about the one major preconvention planning session at which both groups were present: the Lake Villa conference of March 24–25. Mr. Schultz conceded to the jury that the government was not talking about the simple-minded sort of conspiracy in which they would say, "You do that to blow up that" and "I will do that to incite that crowd"; it was talking about "a tacit understanding," "a common design," "a working together." But the jury was not persuaded. It acquitted all seven men on the conspiracy count.

This left the individual counts. Two of the defendants (Froines and Weiner) were charged with teaching and demonstrating the use, application and construction of an incendiary device—namely a firebomb which they allegedly intended to explode in the Grant Park underground garage as a "diversionary" move. But no such explosion ever occurred; no firebombs were ever found; the only "accomplice" apprehended was never brought to trial. The jury acquitted both men on this charge, too.

The other five defendants were separately charged in their individual counts with crossing state lines with intent to incite a riot and then giving a speech or speeches for that purpose. Over and over we heard testimony about those speeches: Jerry Rubin in Lincoln Park saying, "The pigs started the violence, but tonight the people aren't going to give up the park. We have to fight them. They have guns and sticks so we have to arm ourselves with rocks, sticks and everything we can get." Rennie Davis yelling over a bullhorn in Grant Park: "Take the hill. Take the high ground. Don't let the pigs take the hill." Tom Hayden telling the crowd from the Grant Park bandstand: "If blood is going to flow, let's make sure it flows all over this stinking city." Dave Dellinger telling the same crowd a little later, "I'm sure we'll do mobile tactics tonight."

If the defendants had been individually tried under state law for incitement to riot, the state would have had to prove, as the law puts it, that there was a "clear and present danger" that their speeches might cause the demonstrators to riot. But in this trial the government contended that such connections between speech and action were irrelevant. The speeches were important only as proof of intent and the willingness to take some step in furtherance of that intent. The jury found all five men guilty on these counts.

• • •

When the verdict was in, most liberal editorial pages and columnists praised the jury for—alone among all the participants—performing its task well. Time and again, the jurors were singled out for their discrimination and dedication in sorting through the maze of charges and defendants to reach a just decision.

But then jurors began talking about how they had reached their decisions. Those who talked agree that the jury had divided into two camps long before they sat down to deliberate. The camps were remarkably close to what we had speculated all along. One group, which believed all the defendants were guilty on both charges, included Mr. Kratzke, Mr. Nelson, both Mrs. Hill, Mrs. Petersen, Mrs. Burns, Mrs. Bernacki and— the major surprise—Kay Richards. In the other camp, favoring acquittal for all on both charges, were Mrs. Fritz, Mrs. Robbins, Mrs. Seaholm and Mrs. Butler (although Mrs. Butler, ill and eager to get home, defected early).

The deadlock, which lasted almost four days, was broken by Kay Richards, who described her own role as follows: "I acted as mediator. . . . I went back and forth between the two camps, insisting on a verdict. In the end they agreed to compromise, and it was hard for them to do it. Their beliefs hadn't changed as far as guilt or innocence went, and after the verdict there were some of them who wept in anger and frustration. One was almost ill. I cried, too, but only in relief. I

Kay richards

hardly realized it at the time, but I think I am probably the only one of the twelve jurors who is really happy or satisfied with our decision."

Ruth Petersen said: "If it wasn't for that little Katie Richards, I don't know what we would have done. She was wonderful."

Little Katie Richards sold her story of the trial to the Chicago *Sun-Times* for several thousand dollars.

And she deserved it. Mayor Daley could not have pulled off a niftier compromise. Just as the mayor splits the difference between two warring ward bosses, Katie split the difference between the government and the defense. Thanks to her, the verdict was perfectly appropriate: a political end to a political trial.

• • •

Dick Butkus, center linebacker for the Chicago Bears, went down to the Federal Building one day in December to apply for a passport. The Bears had lost again the day before and the beefy Mr. Butkus wasn't feeling very cheerful. So when an equally beefy federal marshal stopped him at the door and asked him to state his business, he said: "None of your business." Four marshals grabbed him and hustled him into the twenty-fourth floor lockup. A half-hour later, he was released with profuse apologies.

Security around the Federal Building was unusually tight throughout the trial. Anybody entering the building was asked his business and had his briefcase or handbag searched. Young people with beards, long hair or unorthodox clothes were questioned longer and often turned away. Spectators lucky enough to get into the courtroom were searched thoroughly and kept under close surveillance. And as soon as court was over, the marshals herded people into the elevators, shouting: "Clear the area."

The marshals were an intriguing lot. The regulars went in for color-coordinated haberdashery—silk shirts, ties, socks and handkerchiefs in Avocado Green, Electric Blue and Strawberry Pink. Some of them made no secret of their distaste for the defendants and their supporters, and when they got a chance to remove one from the courtroom they frequently used unnecessary muscle.

A few of the marshals seemed uncomfortable in the role—among them several black marshals assigned to guard Bobby Seale while he was bound and gagged (for which they were denounced as "pigs"). One noon-time, one of them stood on the plaza downstairs while artists demonstrated against the trial by painting on a huge strip of brown paper. Somebody tossed the marshal a felt-tipped pen and he scrawled in big red letters: "Somewhere there must be a good pig."

• • •

"Are you sure that's the jury's verdict—not guilty?" asked Judge James B. Parsons after Patrolman Thomas M. Mayer was acquitted of beating and threatening a college student during the convention.

When the jury was polled and reaffirmed its verdict, the judge said: "It's unfortunate, under our law, that the government doesn't have the right to a new trial."

Mayer was the seventh Chicago policeman to be acquitted of the charges growing out of the convention disorders (termed a "police riot" by the Walker Commission). The eighth case was later dismissed.

Mr. Kunstler charged during the trial that the government's cases against the policemen were a "sham prosecution," but the U.S. Attorney's office vehemently denied this. "The people who sit on juries in this city are just not ready to convict a Chicago policeman," says Richard Schultz.

• • •

Nearly every noon, Judge Hoffman ate lunch in the men's grill of the Standard Club, Chicago's most elegant Jewish club. The day after he sentenced Bobby Seale, the other lunchers rose and applauded when he walked in.

On January 27, Norman Mailer appeared as a defense witness and was invited to lunch at the club by Jason Epstein, a Random House editor in Chicago to do a book on the trial. Jason invited Jules Feiffer, the cartoonist, and me to join them.

At the last moment, Mailer wanted to eat with Jerry Rubin, Abbie Hoffman and Bill Kunstler. "Bring them along," Jason said with an impish grin.

In the club's lobby, we ran into several obstacles. Abbie and Jerry had no ties. Abbie had no coat, either. And Jason's guest membership couldn't get us all in. So, Abbie and Jerry dashed next door to a haberdasher's and came back with two sober reps. Abbie borrowed a coat from the club barber. And, at the last moment, Saul Alinsky, Chicago's veteran radical organizer, came in with Gordon Sherman, a prominent businessman who contributes to liberal-radical causes. Mr. Sherman, a member, invited us all upstairs.

The headwaiter in the men's grill seated the unusual party without so much as a lifted eyebrow. But Judge Hoffman cast one look of sheer horror, then moved his seat behind a huge pillar.

• • •

"Our strategy was to give Judge Hoffman a heart attack," Jerry Rubin said after the trial. "We gave the court system a heart attack, which is even better."

• • •

On February 17, while waiting for the jury to bring in its verdict, Judge Hoffman heard motions on other cases. One lawyer, who represented a man accused of stealing securities, moved for a six-week postponement of the trial. When the judge asked the reason, the lawyer explained that he was planning a six-week vacation in the Caribbean. Judge Hoffman smiled. Recalling that the lawyer had once been an Assistant United States Attorney, he said, "Now I see why you left your former position here." Then, without further ado, he set a trial date of April 7—the full six-week postponement. It made one wonder what might have happened if Charles Garry had been going to Antigua or Martinique instead of to the hospital for a gall bladder operation.

• • •

"Seen one judge, you've seen 'em all," was the Conspiracy's last slogan. The defendants contend that the judge was no aberration, only the personification of America's judicial system. "Judge Hoffman presides in every court in this country," says Rennie Davis.

The simple answer to that kind of rhetoric is to say it simply isn't so. There are many decent, impartial judges throughout the country who do their best to give defendants a fair trial.

But the trial forced me to reconsider my earlier assumptions about the American judicial system.

104

the jury

Clearly, a federal district court is not always a Temple of Justice. In times like these, white marble and black robes are not enough to insulate courts from the passions which rage outside.

Perhaps it was too much to ask the judicial system to work in a case so blatantly political as this one. Courts were never meant to be political battlegrounds.

But it was the government that chose to fight an essentially political battle in court. Too often people ask whether the judge or the defendants were to blame for politicizing the trial. Undoubtedly, both must bear substantial blame for other things. But the Justice Department and its allies in Chicago must bear this onus. Once that political prosecution was launched, it was probably inevitable that it should be met by an aggressive political defense and presided over by an openly political judge.

Yet we would make a mistake if we dismissed the trial as merely a bizarre freak, consoling ourselves that, after all, the courts work pretty well most of the time. For it is easy enough to maintain due process and constitutional rights in ordinary times and ordinary cases. It is precisely in extraordinary circumstances like these that the court system is put to its ultimate test. Institutions, like people, must be judged on how they react to pressure.

And that, perhaps, is the lesson of these past two years in Chicago. In August 1968, Mayor Daley's political machine met radical protests with a rain of nightsticks. In the winter of 1969, Judge Hoffman's judicial apparatus met challenge with its own form of overreaction. Perhaps our institutions, so imposing in placid times, are too fragile to withstand the shock of confrontation.

• • •

"Santa Barbara, February 26—Governor Ronald Reagan today ordered California's Attorney General to determine whether William M. Kunstler, who spoke here Wednesday shortly before a bank was burned, had crossed state lines with intent to incite a riot."

• • •

On March 15, President Nixon invited Judge Hoffman to a White House prayer breakfast at which Billy Graham delivered the sermon. At a reception afterwards, the judge greeted Treasury Secretary David M. Kennedy, a fellow Chicagoan, as "my banker." Another guest at the affair was Judge Clement F. Haynesworth of South Carolina, the rejected Supreme Court nominee.

• • •

"Chicago, April 3 (AP)—Judge Julius J. Hoffman, who presided in the stormy Chicago trial, again will hear a criminal case involving radical dissenters.

"Judge Hoffman has been assigned the trial of twelve members of the Weatherman faction of the Students for a Democratic Society accused of conspiring to cross state lines to incite rioting in Chicago last October.

"The judge's name came up for the case under the court's random selection method of assigning cases, a clerk for the U.S. District Court said."

About the Author

J. Anthony Lukas graduated from Harvard in 1955, studied at the Free University of Berlin and served with Army Psychological Warfare in Japan. After a four-year apprenticeship on the Baltimore *Sun,* he joined the *New York Times* in 1962, and has served since in the Washington and United Nations bureaus, as a correspondent in Africa and India, as a New York general assignments reporter and as Roving National Correspondent. In 1968 he won the Pulitzer Prize for his story about a girl from Greenwich, Connecticut, who was killed in Greenwich Village. He is now a staff writer for the *New York Times Magazine.*

Design by Gloria Adelson
Set in Linotype Caledonia
Composed by Westcott & Thomson
Printed and bound by The Haddon Craftsmen, Inc.
Harper & Row, Publishers, Inc.